Truly Amazing

Grace

NOEL GRACE

BALBOA.PRESS

A DIVISION OF HAY HOUSE

Balboa Press books may be ordered through booksellers or by contacting:

Balboa Press
A Division of Hay House
1663 Liberty Drive
Bloomington, IN 47403
www.balboapress.com
1 (877) 407-4847

Because of the dynamic nature of the Internet, any web addresses or links contained in this book may have changed since publication and may no longer be valid. The views expressed in this work are solely those of the author and do not necessarily reflect the views of the publisher, and the publisher hereby disclaims any responsibility for them.

The author of this book does not dispense medical advice or prescribe the use of any technique as a form of treatment for physical, emotional, or medical problems without the advice of a physician, either directly or indirectly. The intent of the author is only to offer information of a general nature to help you in your quest for emotional and spiritual well-being. In the event you use any of the information in this book for yourself, which is your constitutional right, the author and the publisher assume no responsibility for your actions.

Print information available on the last page.

ISBN: 978-1-9822-4097-4 (sc)

Balboa Press rev. date: 01/06/2020

May the trumpet sound and the truth be revealed.

VISIONARY

MESSENGER.

2020 EDITION

Contents

Declaration

I will declare that I grew up with my grandmother as an orphan, attended and participated in worshiping God as a seventh day Adventist. When I became an adult I made the decision to get baptized in the cleansing blood of Jesus for the remissions of my sins in a first day Church of God. As time transpired I switched to a first day Baptist, one day I responded to a knock on my front door and it was two first day Jehovah witnesses. Based on what they disclosed I decided to join them as a witness, I then realized that I was not in agreement with their teachings.

They all prayed in Jesus's name and I have a friend that is a Catholic where they pray to Mary asking her to pray for them now and at their passing. Presently I'm not affiliated with any religion but established a personal relationship with God in three dimensions. I spent much time exploring the holy history book where I discovered a lot of information concerning our existence from inception and what is required to acquire everlasting life in paradise. It's my pride and joy to share the things of God much of that information will be disclosed here in this book.

Caution

This is not a religious book although the contents of it is spiritually based and influenced by contents of the holy history book name the bible. It's potent enough to require the capability of discernment and comprehension from the higher power. May the peace of God that is a preservative keep our hearts and minds in Christ, the things of God are trivial to natural humans and it's inconsequential to debate them. It is possible that you'll see repetitions in this venture, it's not intentional but beneficial as it is the adhesive that attaches substance to our minds.

The most vital substance in the perpetuation of our mortal being are air, water and nutrients. God is the owner of our breath and the ruler of our destiny. We must taste and see that God is good and his mercy's endure everlastingly. There are no perfection in the civilization of humanity thereby it's eminent that you may encounter errors in this publication as it was not professionally edited and I'm not a professional typist.

I will inform all my readers that whenever the word God is mentioned in this publication, it's indicating the trinity of God in three dimensions. Father, Son and Spirit all in one accord that existed in the realms of glory before the beginning. Religions teach that our father is in heaven and that's erroneous, the bible was written by several contributors and contain their personal opinions also.

Introduction

I am Noel Grace and originated from the Caribbean island of Jamaica, been a citizen of the USA for thirty six years to date in this year 2020. I'm retired and reside in the Palm beaches of Florida. My main hobbies are reading and meditation because I have resented watching the tube. I spend a large percentage of my time documenting my spiritual inspirations. Blessed is the man that meditate on the things of God day and night, and he will be like a tree planted by the waters of water that bear fruits in its season.

I am a published author of several books and is now at the point that I do not do it for fortune or fame but to provide nutrients for international human minds. I have a large following on social media as I share my inspirations with them daily. This morning I was contacted by an associate who lives in Sierra Leon far in Africa and another in Australia concerning their spiritual experiences.

It was predicted that the words of God will eventually be preached to the entire world in all languages, I can only speak English but hope that sometime in the not distant future I will be able to afford to have translations done of my books to all nations. I have the privilege to make my requests be made known to the source of my existence so in that case here's one.

Dedication

This publication is designed to be a stairway in the process of expanding the kingdom of God on this earth as it is in heaven. I dedicate it primarily to our maker, provider and the source of our existence. Secondly to my 5,000 + associates on social media, my children and other family and friends including the readers of my publications. The most recent publications are "Visions for our Mission" @ Xlibris.com and "Authenticity" @ Iegaiabooks.com.

May God give us the desires of our hearts according to his will, and I am certain that his promises are sure. I will reiterate when God is mentioned we are interacting with a trinity composed of the father Jehovah God, Christ the Lord, God, Word, Truth, and Way. Holy the Spirit/ God all in one. I will not recommend approaching the throne of grace with a shopping list in Jesus name.

As you penetrate the contents of this book do not allow yourself to be deterred by me mentioning God as he is the source of our existence, be persistent and absorb the entire book. I will caution everyone to be careful as there are pitfalls in the venture of life, and not become victims if we are lacking in knowledge. In this age when the main source of information is on the world wide web known as the internet you must acquire the capability of discernment.

I dedicate this publication to the entire humanity in an effort to get our minds prepared for the negative trends based on the direction things are heading. There are several different media involved in the process, like texting, e-mailing and social medias. We must be cautious based on the credibility of the substance we acquire, it's imperative that we are able to evaluate it's accuracy. It's a known fact that in order to make the right decisions the information must be processed by our hearts to be credible.

I will now imply that you are heading in a none-fiction environment as the contents of this book are true realities of life. It's of vital importance to seek and acquire potent substance mainly through literature to nurture and maintain a sound mental heart and mind. Always insist on projecting a profile of solidarity, utilizing eloquent implications to acquire respect from others in the arena of life.

You are now released to do an exploration and attain the impact on your mental faculties as intended initially. We will meet at the culmination of this publication and I anticipate your complements.

Things of God

The contents of this publication were derived from sources explored by the author to include abstracts from the only holy history book for an international audience. This book was designed by it's author not to be instructional but motivational as a monument for reference to verify the things of God. There have been documented references available and utilized by several generations for centuries containing predictions and instructions that have been manifested.

As we go along here I will request that you use your capability of discernment to comprehend the contents of this publication as it's named. It was predicted that without knowledge people will perish because of ignorance that creates vulnerability whereby they become victims of the evil adversary. We are accustomed to initiate all processes at the beginning but in this endeavor I will commence before the beginning as the beginning signifies timing.

I will inform you that God the father Jehovah, his son Christ, Lord, Word, Way and Truth including Holy the Spirit/ God existed as a trinity in the realms of glory before the beginning of time. The first creation was the universe with all the numerous planets including the heaven and earth. The planet heaven is occupied by invisible spirits called the angelic force of God with Michael the archangel in command.

The preceding will awake your knowledge that Christ is not the surname of Jesus as they are two separate spirits, Christ is a member of the trinity and Jesus is affiliated with it but not a member of it, thereby he cannot access the realms of glory where the main administrator exist. The earth was put in rotation on a timer by God, hence the beginning of time and unto this day the clock keeps ticking.

The time came when the trinity had a conference and decided to

1

create two humans a male named Adam and a female named Lilleath with the charactaristics of God. Eve was not involved as she was not created but made from the dust of the earth to be a companion for Adam, to go multiply and inhabit the earth which was later named the world. God is a God of order, precision and authority and there came a time in the process that he put it on hold.

In the mean time back on the spiritual planet one of the angels defected and was named Lucifer meaning a evil oposition to God. Lucifer approached Eve and deceived her to disobey the ordinance of God so he implanted a human seed in her, after the time of development of the fetus Eve delivered a set of twins male and female. The name of the male was Cain and the female Luluwah and she was very attractive.

Adan copulated with Eve when the process restarted and she was impregnated now with Adam's seed. As time went by the fetus developed and it was time for delivery and she again produced another set of twins male named Able and a female named Acklia. Over time when all four children matured and were ready for mating the parents made sure that they did not mate with their birthmate. What they did was to cross them so Able got the more attractive sister and that got Cain jealous.

The reason for his jealousy was that he attained the lesser attractive sister. There is something complicated here as no one knew of the whereabouts of Lilleth the female God created, the assumption was that she migrated to some distant land and was confronted by Lucifer as what happened to Eve. Here we go again, Able was missing for some time and Cain was questioned as to his brother's whereabouts and he denied having any knowledge of it..

It was eventually discovered that Cain killed his brother in the field because of jealousy and ran off to a land called Nod, where he found himself a wife. As they were the only humans on that earth it was assumed that the female that Cain married was a descendant of Lilleth. Lucifer had undeserved privileges whereby he had access to both heaven and on earth where until this day can access the human mental faculties with deceptions and devise hindrances.

There was a time when things got beyond the level of the tolerance of God and he decided to cleanse the earth. The decision was made by the trinity to do a cleansing of the earth by water. There was a man by the name of Noah who had a family that was living right in the sight of God. The decision was made to use him to carry out an assigned mission to build a boat like vessel to float on water called the ark.

Noah was instructed as to the procedure to prepare for a flood, before the rain started he was supposed to load on all his sons and their wives and several species of live animals in existence. Noah obeyed God and the rain started for days and the earth was totally flooded but the ark with its occupants survived. When the rain stopped and all the water receded there was a cleansed new earth. The ark landed and unloaded all the occupants and it was a new beginning.

Although the earth was cleansed humans still contained the sins inherited from the forefathers as far back as Eve and Cain. Eventually God devised the means to rescue them from it. This was the way Jesus came into existence and he is significant in the equation, we give thanks to God for the cleansing blood of Jesus that save us from our sins as long as we accept that privilege. As it was predicted that the Word would become flesh and dwell among us as a human on this earth, but Jesus was not the word.

A virgin from a family of God was engaged to marry a man named Joseph. But she was identified to be utilized to accomplish the assignment of bringing a child into this world and Holy the Spirit of the trinity implanted a small portion of Christ as a human seed inside the virgin Mary and impregnated her. All of us humans were made through a process and so was Jesus. The account of his appearance and the circumstance under which it was disclosed in the holy book in several aspects especially the weather in that part of the earth at that time of the year.

At that time when it occurred it was skeptical but there are no alternatives to resort to assumptions. Jesus was the son of man, a fruit of the womb of Mary and consisted of all the contents that we all consisted of. He had a body, mind, spirit, being and soul like we all possess. The time now that is celebrated for the arrival of Jesus is a time that the weather is extremely cold and wet. According to the account recorded he was born in a manger where animals were.

While shepherds were watching their flocks in the night all were seated on the ground, that's extreme. It's my responsibility as a visionary messenger to identify portions of the inconsistencies, misconceptions and faulty perceptions recorded in the holy book. Here is a prevalent one, the only all-mighty God, everlasting father and prince of peace is Jehovah. Christ the Lord son of God. Word and Holy the Spirit is a trinity. It's stipulated in the holy book that after the birth an angel made the announcement.

Stating that unto us a son is born and a child given and his name will be called mighty God, everlasting father, king of kings and prince of peace. It was also stated that the iniquity of us all will be on his shoulder. It's of utmost importance that we identify these errors to be on the right track. The earth was created as a round globe and in the book it's mentioned that the earth have four corners not directions. Heaven is one of the planets God created in the universe occupied by invisible spirits known as the angelic force of God.

Although God the father is omnipresent he is not an occupant of heaven Christ with Jesus are. The contents of the holy book was compiled from inputs by several contributors and served as a guide for humanities for centuries. There was no documentations of most of Jesus's childhood until his ministry began, he did marvelous things including raising Lazarus from the dead. He healed the sick, restore visions to the blind and several other deeds as he was accompanied and empowered by Holy the Spirit.

None of the spirits of the trinity of God ever uttered words but they spoke through Jesus and now us authors by inspirations. The enormous universe declare the glory of God and the firmaments displays his handy works. Because it became hectic on Jesus in his ministry he appointed twelve disciples to assist him in doing the will of the father. Time and time again he mentioned that it's the father that sent him and what he did was not according to his will but the will of the father and it must be done.

I rarely mention the evil adversary Lucifer here as I'm not here to promote his agenda, but it's of vital importance that we are all aware of his antics. He devised an industry name religions and there are numerous amounts of them and there foundation is based on the holy book in different versions and languages. There is no unity among them as they are grossly divisive and loaded with deceptions to mislead the world to be claimed by him based on lack of the truth.

We were instructed to search and get to know the truth to be set free from the bondage of the adversary. At this point in time I will declare to you that Christ/God the Truth, Lord, Word from before the beginning. When it was disclosed that Jesus was the Messiah they decided to kill him so they went in search of him. One of his disciples was a son of Lucifer his name was Judas. Regardless Jesus taught the other disciples spiritual rituals that should be done like baptism and the Lord supper.

The practice of submersion under water signifies being washed in the cleansing blood of Jesus to wash away the sins of this world, to become children of God. The evening meal signifies the breaking of the bread being his body and the wine being his blood again. Eventually he was identified by Judas and they captured and took disadvantage of him physically. At the final stage of destruction they placed a thorn on his head, pierced his sides and crucified him then hanged him on a stake between two thieves.

The blood of Jesus was shed at Calvary, he was taken down and buried and in three days he conquered death and was transformed to be a spirit and was ascended into heaven to be with Christ in one accord. The father was well pleased of his accomplishment that he begotten him as his only adopted son. The first action Jesus took was to confiscate the passport of Lucifer to stop him from entering heaven so he cannot pollute the angels and changed his name to Satan.

Who am I to question the things of God it's not my intent, I am only a visionary messenger. I am amazed that the evil adversary is permitted to roam this earth, interact with the world and have access to human mental faculties. Presently he is in the process of and pollute the entire humanity to accompany him to the lake of fire. I perceive him as being omnipresent as one of my social media associate in Lagos Nigeria in Africa informed me of his encounter with him there.

The only place he cannot access is heaven as his passport was confiscated by Jesus when he got there as he encountered him here on this earth. As it was in the beginning, so will it be in the end. It is also substantial to seek and acquire a copy of my recent book "Vision for our mission" by Noel Grace @ Xlibris.com and absorb the substance in the contents of it. You will be blessed to an enormous mental proportion by the power of the most high.

The information I'm sharing here with you are vital for your being, there are people among us that are wolves in sheep clothing. It's best for them to get out from among us and seek alternatives. A large percentage of humanity are deceived by the doctrines taught by religions, with the false hope of going to heaven and glory. Most of the utterances of Jesus when he walked this earth was Christ speaking through him as he was a part of him.

Misconceptions was the order of the day and is deceiving the vulnerable humans among us, due to lack of knowledge of the truth. One of the most frequent deception is trying to approach the throne of grace to communicate with God in the names of Jesus and his mother Mary. Jesus is affiliated with God but he is not a member of the trinity so he is not God. There is only way is in spirit and in truth by way of Christ the true son of Almighty God Jehovah the father.

We must open the doors of our spiritual hearts to accept the gift of God and get submerged in the blood of Jesus to acquire eternal life. God is stringent concerning his laws, principles, processes, promises and compliances with his ten commandments. The morning after midnight and the evening was the first day and it was named Sunday. There are seven days in a week, it was stipulated in the holy book that we humans should toil for six days and rest on the seventh and keep that day holy.

During the process of God's creations Jesus was not present as he had to be made through the process that us humans come through. Christ the Word who is a member of the trinity of God was present and the Word, Lord, Way and Truth the one and only way to access the father. I will give God honor, glory, thanks and praise by way of Christ until my last breath as he owns my breath and rules my destiny.

I recommend that we all join together, keep the commandments of God to be with Christ and Jesus on the new earth name eternal paradise. Until that time comes we must worship the Lord in the beauty of holiness as his joy is our strength. At this time I will make my request be made known to the Lord to give us strength to face another day and help us to carry our heavy mantel burdens of life.

May we have peace on this earth, it's eminent that the system of things that was devised and implemented by the evil adversary is on the verge of collapsing. It's now time to do a healing of all humanity to awaken their minds to consciousness to make a total U-turn and head in the right direction. Exploitation is the tool being used by nations with resource and sustained by technology to take disadvantage of other nations. It was predicted that the time will come when nation will rise against nations.

By utilizing the power of technology the USA sent astronauts to investigate the planet moon and verified that humans exist on no other planet but this earth. The tears from our eyes is a liquidation of our emotions, there are tears of sadness originated from the mind caused by dissatisfaction, hurt and death. There are tears of joy accompanied with laughter that originates from our hearts caused by successful accomplishments, rewards and satisfaction.

Let us all make the joy of the Lord be our strength, seasons comes and seasons go, when the going gets tough that's when we need a friend. We do have the privilege to have a friend in Jesus who will bear all our sorrows and troubles to heal our wines. Here is the sequence of authority, God the father Jehovah is God of all gods and the chief executive like a main frame computer, he does all the monitoring and guidance like the captain of a ship but he is in glory land not in heaven.

Holy the Spirit and God is like a police department that enforces all the laws and guidelines with power and might, he is always available twenty four seven so we can call on him anytime. Christ is the real deal he is our all in all our refuge and strength in times of storm. Christ inherited Jesus as his assistant and representative to be with him through eternity as he is a part of him. Our God in three dimension within the realms of glory is truly amazing beyond the comprehension of humanity and is worthy of our praise.

May the grace of God that promote all comprehension preserve our hearts and minds by Christ, we must give the Lord praise and approach the throne of grace to communicate with the father of all creation by way of Christ. It is of vital importance that we acquire consciousness by attaining wisdom from knowledge of the truth. We will not comply with the council of the ungodly or indulge in sinfulness and we will be rewarded greatly by our maker. Christ is our only Lord and we must all lift his name on high.

We must sing a new song of praise to God with the melodious sounds of instruments we give thanks for our breath, grace, peace, love, joy, blessings and mercy. Our soul is the most valuable asset of our being and we were given the opportunity to make the choice for it's final destination. Christ and Jesus are in the process of preparing a new eternal paradise here on the new earth as spirits and they will be there to welcome us.

God have never been an human, Holy the Spirit who is God took a small portion of Christ who is God transformed it to be a human seed and implanted it in the virgin Mary. Jesus was born in flesh as a son of man and a fruit of the womb of Mary his mother. He did a marvelous accomplishment of his assignments and made the father Jehovah well pleased. The father made him his only begotten son, Jesus was eventually crucified for us to get remission from our sins both inherited and committed.

He conquered death by rising on the third day, He was then transformed to be a spirit and ascended to heaven to be with Christ. Jesus is not a member of the trinity of God meaning he is not God but a representative of Christ. Religions promote spiritual diversity, there's only one true and living God Almighty in three dimensions, the contents of the bible is what all religions rely on for directives and it's inconsistent in nature but I respect it. The religions were devised by the evil adversary as a business.

It's recently been diagnosed as one of the most successful business ventures as most of its leaders are very wealthy. Religion is a multi-billion dollar business, they have discovered that the manufactured disease called cancer is a business. I will categorize religion as a mental cancer induced by the evil adversary. Presently The entertainment industry in 2020 is running out of money whereby a lot of the entertainers are getting saved to go where the money is. Recently I read of a saved entertainer collecting money to enter his church.

The first creation of God was the universe with all it's planets including heaven and the earth, heaven is a unique planet consisting of only the spiritual angelic forces of God including Jesus with Michael the archangel in command. Jesus is omnipresent meaning he's here on this earth in control of humanity and empowered by Christ and Holy the Spirit. God in three dimensions then spoke to us through the mortal Jesus then, heaven is not being prepared for us as religions teach because it's been there.

This present earth will eventually be cleansed with fire and when it's cooled off we will join Christ and Jesus in eternal paradise here. At this point in my assignment I will reiterate my appeal to all humanity not to allow themselves to be indoctrinated by religions with the false hope of going to heaven or glory. Do not indulge in world politics resist it as it's a domain devised by the evil adversary to mislead us, concentrate on the things of God.

Our God is an awesome God in three dimensions, he's precisely systematic and function in sequences. Humanity is at the mercy of God, Jesus the only begotten son of God and the inferior evil adversary. The two main priorities are the expansion of God's kingdom on planet earth as it is on planet heaven. Second in the sequence is the acquisition of human souls, the most valuable commodity. Due to the goodness and mercy of God, humanity was given the privilege to make a choice.

Blessed be the Lord God Almighty he reign forever and more, from everlasting and beyond our God have no beginning and no end. Come taste and see that the Lord is good and his mercies endure through all generations. May his goodness and mercy follow and protect us for all the days of our lives. Christ is Lord/God/Son of God/ Word/Way and our all in all is original. Christ was not created, made or born.

Anyone that aspire being in the secret place of the most high is secure. In the hands of the Almighty like a hen sitting on her eggs to keep them worm. Be informed that heaven is not a place of refuge it's one of the planets in the universe occupied by spirits. The universe is not the heavens, there's only one spiritual planet named heaven. The implication that God's kingdom will come on earth as it is in heaven is referring to paradise is being prepared for human souls.

Let us make a joyful noise unto the Lord and get in his presence with singing sweet redemption songs of praise. The joy of the Lord is our strength, let's worship him in the beauty of holiness. Here I am again reiterating the recipe designed by God as I'm being confronted by religious readers of my books. God is our maker and sustainer, he's the only true God, a trinity comprising of the father, son and spirit. For God so live this world that he sent his only begotten/adopted son Jesus to rescue us from our sin debt.

Jesus was a son of man as he was a fruit of the womb of is mother the virgin Mary who was a human, he did a marvelous accomplishments of his assignments. While Jesus was on this earth as a human doing the will of the father, God spoke to us through his utterances and eventually his blood was shed on Calvary to save us. As I mentioned earlier that God is completed trinity. Jesus conquered death was transformed and ascended to heaven as a spirit, but is not god as religions project him to be.

Christ the son of God and God, Lord, Truth and Way is the only way to communicate with the father, not in Jesus's name. I'm sure there will be religious people to disagree but I'm convinced that God is using me as a Jonah.

The Realities of Mortality

Whenever we walk through storms don't fear hold our heads up high and do not be afraid of atrocities, put our trust in the Lord and he will be there with us. The race is not for the swift but for who can endure to the finish line. It's not the size of the gun that determines the damage that can be done it's the effect of the bullet, always follow the leader closely to get there. It is inconsequential to memorize the past as its history it's more productive to anticipate a brighter future like night turn to day.

It's beneficial to choose to be a possession of God and become a sheep of his pasture. At no time should we allow anyone to endanger our chosen destiny as its ruled by God. The container that's named hope have holes in it called uncertainties, it's best to seek security in the Lord and stand on him as the solid rock. May goodness and mercy from the Lord follow us all the days of our lives as it's our desire to be in his house forever.

Cherish and give thanks to the Lord for all our possessions and seek ways to improve them. It's better to have a live mouse than a dead lion. I'm calling on all who are within the boundaries of my influence who have not made the commitment yet to be a part of the kingdom of God on this earth to act now before it's too late. It's time to submit your entire being to God and get submerged in the cleansing blood of Jesus, so your name will be written in the lambs book of life.

We should make sure that when our name is called up yonder we'll be there to answer, get ready. None of my perceptions are critical or divisive instead they are meant to be implemented, and be correctional for cultivating unity in the process of expanding God's kingdom here on earth as it is in heaven. Seek first the kingdom and all its righteousness and all other

11

necessities will be added as blessings. Let us all worship God in the beauty of holiness through Christ with Jesus in one accord empowered by holiness in the Spirit, one God in three dimensions.

All major constructed monumental places of worship by different religions are decorated with a cross signifying Jesus died on a cross, he was crucified and hanged on a stake between two thieves. A large percentage of religions keep telling humanity that Jesus is coming soon so it creates paranoia like when an hurricane is approaching for people to put up shutters. Always let the words of our mouth and the meditations of our heart be acceptable to God.

God is our refuge and strength a present help in times of trouble we should put our trust in him. Our mental heart is the traffic light of our being, always wait on its directives to proceed. Before making any decision always get the subconscious mind involved and when it's done it then send it to the heart to be pondered. Eventually it reaches the conscious mind to be executed.

May we come to the realization that life is not a bed of roses, there are rivers to cross and mountains to climb overlooking the valleys. The train of life keep moving right along one day at a time, we must make hay while the sun is shining and seek shelter when it rains. It's of utmost importance that we utilize the limited allotment of our time in this process until we reach our ultimate destination based on our choice.

This book is designed to be a life's manual if at any time it seem you are going out of your comfort zone, flip the page and continue to reap the benefits of your investment. There will be times that you will be required to make adjustments to your mental paradigms for the contents of this media to help make the necessary changes in your life pursuit. There will be moments when issues seem unrealistic, just sit back and enjoy the experience. There will be treats and humor, pleasure and discomfort with food for the mind.

May our hearts be activated and coordinated for this process, one will be pondering while the other pumps blood through your veins to suffice the body functions. I will encourage you to timely absorb the contents of this media as there will be enormous amount of material targeted for your mental faculties. There will come times when it seem controversial, that is great as controversy generates interest, activates curiosity and eventually alleviates boredom. There is no perfection in civilization so it's evidently you will encounter errors in this dialogue, overlook them and move on.

We do have to acknowledge realities, for example truth also called facts are absolute thereby it's inconsequential to dispute or debate them. Realities are the elements that impacts our lives in general and unpredictable in nature. In most cases due to circumstances we can do nothing but to activate our tolerance and endure the duration. A very potent aspect of our being is our belief system, as the evil adversary devised ways to deceive us through religions.

It's of vital importance that we are aware of what's going on around us and position ourselves to encounter the circumstances to prevail. Realities and misconceptions are relevant but not related as they come in different packages. Here are some of the attires in witch misconceptions is dressed in cults, lodges, fraternities, ideologies, religions and other extremities. Vulnerability is cultivated through ignorance which is an element of subjection, anything that comes along there is always someone to participate in it.

In the entertainment arena there are people making signs for association with the substance of the almighty dollar in the USA and do not know the meaning of it. They are like playing with fire, one guy told me what to look for on the one dollar bill and I checked it out and anticipate trouble in the future. Ideologies enhanced by technology are becoming involved in all aspects of our existence and in dangerous internationally. There are people encountering daily stress due to faulty decisions they made.

Realities is not comprised of proto-types there are several types of reality, some are temporary while others are permanent based on circumstances and timing. Predators, receptors and loan sharks are all brothers and related to the parasite family, be careful not to be a victim of them. Always indulge and operate in moderation, do not spend more than you earn, spend your resources on what you need and not on what you want.

Do not try to imitate the lifestyle of others substances or resources as you are not aware of how they acquired them. There are people declaring bankruptcy because they went overboard. Although you may be in too deep there is never a time when you cannot make a U-turn and head in the right direction. At this point in this dialogue I will make you be aware of the downward progression of our lives called aging, the journey of life is like using a ladder to climb to the top of a mountain, and is compelled to descend back to the bottom of it all.

If you are a young adult I will advise you to acquire at least one child to be there for you when you get to the bottom. There will be signs along the way just like you are on a adventurous excursion, there are times that you will be aware of the deterioration involved in the process. Do not try to ignore or disregard any symptoms, pay attention and seek medical assistance. In most cases the first organ attracted is the heart pump, that's critical and in some cases if not treated early cause us to depart life prematurely although I believe in destiny.

Two of the most profitable and wealthy industries in this world are religions and drug/medication sources. In the religion industry the evil adversary appoint ministers, pastors, priests and others to capitalize in the selling of Jesus's name to mostly the unfortunate and disadvantaged ones among us. they acquire resource mainly by collecting offerings, tithes, donations and gifts. From my seat in the pavilion here in the US I observe leaders who became million years wealthy, some even travel on private jet plains.

Recently I read of a ninety two year old female being expelled from her congregation due to getting behind on her tithes, I was amazed. On the other side of the coin it's more disadvantageous, as due to the population explosion the food that we consume is like poisoned. Most of the foods available to us are infested with human destructive chemicals on one side and the other side are the meats. The most common and inexpensive meat is chicken that grows with artificial corn and other chemically infested foods.

Chickens from the time they are hatched from eggs to when they are on the table for consumption is approximately three to four weeks. Please be patient we are not there yet, the drug industry is so enormously large to the extent where they are importing imitations of the drugs from inexpensive overseas sources. The overseas drugs are named generics and is utilized as substitute on us humans,

Our bodies consist of numerous organs to sustain our natural existence and the main one is our head consisting of the main command center with our mental heart, mind, brain, spirit and will. The first organ that gets attacked is our heart pump caused by what our digestive system acquire. There are incidents where the life of people leave here prematurely, these are all complicated realities. I am convinced that all lives have a blue print and predestined as we all have an appointment with the eminent death.

As I mentioned earlier about the numerous amount of organs in our body's working in a sequence, as we get older deterioration set in thereby certain organs begin to fail. The USA is a grossly populated continent so based on the preceding disclosures in order to heal and maintain life another industry developed. It's called the healthcare services, this is a multi-million dollar industry and is primarily supervised and controlled by the human body mechanics known as doctors.

The doctors make the diagnosis and prescribe the medications to counteract or heal us the patients, there are people with a medication list of as much as fifteen medicines per day. There are large land compounds with huge monuments called hospitals that accommodates ill patients. This healthcare industry get most of its wealth from insurance companies and the patients are required to pay a portion called copayments. The hospitals have a staff of nurses with assistant nurses, specialists, laboratory technicians and numerous other employees in different departments.

Whenever we get out of those institutions they harass us with bills in the mail. My advice to you is to enjoy now, try to avoid getting into situations to cause you pain and loss of sleep. It's better to enjoy what we have acquired now than for someone else to do it for you when you are gone. God is in total control of our destiny so we need to do the right things in the duration of life. Seek ways of having fun and laughter joy and peace, sharing is caring do not be selfish in your doings so give an helping hand when you can.

Always be prepared and determined to make all our endeavors achievable regardless of the obstacle's we encounter. In our life pursuit if someone should ask how is our day going, the response should always be positive because we can make it that way. Our life is not like a Ferris-wheel it does have intervals and as we get older we will realize that there are things we used to do that we cannot do anymore. Although the road seem rocky at times put on your armor and stay the course for its duration.

A gift is a wonderful thing and is welcomed with gratitude, in most cases it is in material or financial forms. I discovered that the most expensive gift ever given was Jesus who was sacrificed so his cleansing blood can save us all from our inherited and committed sins. By his stripes we are healed if we accept that gift. Patience is a virtue that lightens the mental overload on our minds, I will not take credit for being a patient individual and can remember back in my younger days when all my patients were in the hospital.

There are some very impatient people among us for sure and they create confrontations, like people that have the habit of cutting lines. I witness some time ago in a parking lot where man was waiting patiently for someone to leave so he could get the spot. Eventually someone left and a female from nowhere drive in it totally disregarding the man waiting. That caused major disturbance and there were some strong verbal utterances exchanged, it's very hurtful when people do things like those.

We are living in a time when some people only think about themselves, I had an incident where I had to pinch myself to be sure I'm visible. We must realize that we are living in an environment controlled by time so we have to make the necessary adjustments. Consider others so we do not cause any discomfort, we all can live as one in peace and harmony. We are living in a time when people especially ladies, are dissatisfied with there outward appearance and there are industries that developed to make the necessary adjustments.

There is a sexual practice called homosexuality and it's practiced by both male and female, there is a female acquaintance of mine that has a female mate. What they did was to have a seed from a male implanted inside the mate and she had a female child and claim that she is the father. There are males changing their personality to be females and likewise females doing the same. It's like getting crazy out there in the field of satisfaction. In my research of the holy history book I saw the similar deeds in the previous world.

It's like they are teasing God to cleanse this earth again, but it will all be done in his time. Life is like going on an excursion on a one way highway, there are no second chances but we do have choices to make, we can be what we desire to be. There is an element of life whereby we are required to make decisions, if we make bad ones we suffer the consequences and if we make good ones we reap the benefits. We are at a critical stage of existence, God planned it that there should be relationships become a union in the process of making a family.

Have you ever wonder why when males are getting aged the hair in the middle of their heads thins out and sometimes eventually go totally bald ?. Here is the reality, because our conscious minds are in an absorption mode it operates under vacuum so the older we get is the more curious we become. The main computer that controls the functions of our bodies is in our heads and called the brain that acquire substance from our senses. At the top of our head is where the antenna is seeking information to feed the brain and satisfy its curiosity.

Sometimes we see men that are totally bald, that does not mean that they are smarter than normal, I wish that was the case. In the mix there are truth, lie, good, bad, deceptions, misconceptions, religions, indoctrinations and other negatives available for ignorant and vulnerable humans. Presently baldness is a popular style, even younger folks dress up without hair on their heads. I'm sure you have heard the saying that iron sharpens iron, that's the purpose of my mission to wake you up from your slumber to initiate a new beginning.

I hope you are absorbing what you are reading and act on it it's potent stuff, if you plant a seed and do not give it water it will not grow. There are rules of God, rules of man and rules of nature, recently I ran into a set of rules I was not aware of. I will share them with you I am sure there will be disagreements in this dialogue based on your knowledge of the facts. Beliefs, comprehension, indoctrination and other things you have encountered that polluted your mental faculties can be eliminated.

Here we go with the laws I encountered and promised to share with you.

1. If you spit in the sky it will fall right back in your eyes.
1. If you don't go under a tree birds will not be able to dump on you.
2. While working on your car and your hands get greasy that's when …. the phone will ring or you will feel like peeing.

3. You will not get a busy signal if you dial a wrong number.
4. If you tell your boss you had a flat tire, that's why you are late, you ... bet your life saver you will get one the next morning.
5. If you change lanes on the hi-way to go faster, you can bet that lane will go by you.
6. You will always meet someone important when you are with a less important person.
7. Whenever you try to prove something does not work, that's when it works.
8. The severity of an itch on your back is usually always out of reach.
9. Anything can happen in a conversation when the participants are ignorant of the facts.

The pathway of life is cluttered with obstacle's, it is up to us to decide if they are stumbling blocks or stepping stones, I will imply the following.

1. Happiness will keep us sweet with joy and laughter.
2. Trials with the joy of the Lord will keep us strong.
3. Sorrow will keep us down in sadness, but there's hope.
4. Success will keep us growing, indulge in caring and sharing.
5. Only God can keep us going, if you trust in him.

The thought process is very important to utilize positively to enhance our patience to tolerate the realities of life. One of my associates confided in me and disclosed that he does not believe in God that told me that he is walking in the council of the ungodly and the pathway of sinners. I was disappointed but all I could do was to sympathize with him and hope someday he will come to realize the source of his existence.

I discovered my capability of being a published author in the latter stage of my life and find it amazing also rewarding especially when I see people responding to the contents of my books. This book is very unusual because it causes us to concentrate on the realities of life and open our awareness of the existence of our being and the sustainer of it all. Our mind is similar to a umbrella or parachute, it operate best when it's open. The grass always seem greener on the other side, until when the rubber meets the road and we get there to face reality.

Based on my research of the holy history book called the bible, I have concluded that it's very credible and factual based on the documentations and accomplishments of it's contents. It was culminated at the book of Revelation centuries ago and there is no knowledge of any continuation in terms of directives for modern civilization. What's going on now is that this world is going in the wrong direction whereby in a short distant in time it will be destructive for humanity.

It's obvious that was not the way God planned it, it all commenced when the evil adversary devised and implemented the religious industry. Primarily by having humanity trying to access the throne of grace to communicate with the father by the wrong way. When Jesus was here on this earth he possessed all the components of all us humans and was accompanied by Holy the Spirit and did not become a spirit until after his resurrection. God is a spirit in three dimensions and Jesus is not a member of the trinity.

All spirits are invisible and cannot utter or die, all documented accounts of God's commands and directives even his commandments were documented by way of inspirations through Jesus and other contributors to include song writers, poets, prophets, authors and several others until this day. There's no accounts of God himself verbally issued any command or instructions. If there is anywhere in the bible that it's mentioned that God said anything it would be error nous.

This planet earth is a vineyard for the survival of humanity, associate with others and advocate the acquisition of potent substance. We were all placed here to accomplish a mission meaning we do have a purpose, no one know what their purpose is but some time in our existence we will do something significant to substantiate it. I do appreciate your participation in this venture and will complement you for your patience and tolerance in the acquisition of knowledge of the realities of life for its duration.

Joy is a precious commodity that is acquired through our mental perceptions to enhance our hope in living a meaningful life, hope is the beginning of wisdom from the Lord. It's of paramount importance that we devise and maintain a fruitful anticipation of a prosperous accomplishment. Based on my decision I've submitted my entire being to my creator to be utilized for his purpose that his will be done. Always trust in the Lord with all your spiritual heart and not your understanding and he will direct your pathway.

Sleeping is a process of resting and a journey but no one know their destination, always give thanks to our sustainer at the dawning of each new day. We all were all given the capability to produce substance for the duration of our existence except the disabled ones among us. Always be compassionate and help to satisfy genuine needs, be sure that your conservative agenda doesn't curtail your generosity and compassion. Endeavor in sowing productive seeds to benefit the needs of the unfortunate ones.

My advice to you is to make the best of your life carefully as you know not when it will end, although I'm convinced that all human's life is predestined. It was appointed to all of us to die but when we go that's not it, there's another realm that welcome us with two compartments. One is controlled by our maker and the other by the evil adversary, we do have the privilege of making the choice of which one we go.

Presently the perpetuation of our lives have become a business whereby there are poisonous defections developed in laboratories that are induced in whoever is vulnerable. There is a health care industry whereby chemical and drugs are used by doctors in the name of healing, of course there are the morticians standing in line to make their money also for the funerals of the nonesurvivers.

At this point I must wish you a happy birthday as this is the first day in the rest of your life. Oh how good and pleasant it is for us all to live in peace, love and harmony, life is not a bed of roses there are rivers to cross and mountains to climb overlooking the valleys of desperation. My two main wishes are that I will dwell in the house of the Lord forever in paradise and will meet you all on that beautiful shore.

Facts of Life

At this moment we will get prepared for a mental excursion as we will be exercising our minds in the changing of the course some of us are on. Two valuable assets that we possess are our demeanor and presentation, we will never get a second chance to make a first impression. I will remind you that it's the peace of God that passes all understanding and preserve our hearts and minds for the duration of our lives, seek and acquire it. I can remember an incident while I was out with my youngest daughter.

I observed an homeless man in front of a food store talking to himself and I gave my daughter five dollars to give him, immediately he went inside the store and came out with some food and started consuming it. My daughter then looked at me in amazement and said, dad how did you know that man was hungry? I told her I was informed by the spirit and she was impressed. Here's another one, there was an old lady that lived next door to an ungodly old man and one day the lady was praying to God for food and the man heard.

The man went to the store and bought some food and gave it to her, she expressed her appreciation to him then said thanks to God. The man was upset and told her it was not God who got her the food it was him, he didn't realize he was being used to do the will of God. Life is a wonderful thing if you make it just that and no in-between, the quality of our lives relies on the quality of our thoughts. Do not rely on anyone to give you happiness nor seek material things to sustain it.

It is a good practice to diversify and do not rely on any source other than God, there will be times when the candle burn out and you can revert. It's beneficial to interact and utilize the sub-folders of our conscious minds and use them productively like innovations, imagination and anticipation and we will be rewarded. We all have a level of tolerance so it's perfectly normal and healthy to cry and release tensions, when our feelings are hurt. There's no American dream, that fantasy make people go seeking to acquire fortune like dogs chasing birds, and the rest is history.

An associate gave me some lessons in English that I was not aware of and I was astonished as that's the only language that I speak. There a lot of technicalities that I'm not aware of and failed at the test. It's totally incorrect to say I are or I is but yours truly is skillful enough to override it, check this out I is the number nine letter in the English alphabet and I know a guy that his name initials are IR perfect English, so you see that codes can be broken.

My request at this time is that you put your heart in a pondering mode, there are no eggs in eggplant, nor ham in hamburger neither is there any pine in pine apple.

English muffins were not invented in England nor French fries in France. I hope you are dancing to the beat.

Boxing rings are square and guinea pigs are not from Guinea nor are they pigs.

A slim chance and a fat chance are similar but a wise man and a wise guy are opposites.

A house can burn up while it buns down and you can fill in a form by filling it out.

Computers were created by the human race without being involved in a competition.

Sweet breads are not sweet because they are meats to be enjoyed in a taste full meal.

There are words that are spelt the same but have different meanings like bass which is a fish was painted on a bass meaning tone drum meaning a tone drum.

Since there is no time like the present it's time to present the gift to its recipient.

The boy shot at the dove and it dove in the bushes to escape any chance of being hurt.

When the garbage truck got to the dump it was so full that they had to refuse the refuse.

Why is it that writers write but fingers do not fing, grocers do not grose and hammers do not ham.

Let's get back to normalcy here, the human body is very complicated simply because we were made with the characteristics of Almighty God. I will not apologize to you if you are not a God fearing being. Our body is an elaborate power plant that generates electronic pulses to enhance the process in the function of our mortal being. There are nutritiona required to sustain the different faculties. There is a spiritual side of our existence and on a regular basis we must recognize it and give appreciation for our privileges.

Ever since I got the assignment to write and publish this book it's like a flood gate open with substantial information to be documented. Sharing it with this audience which I anticipate will meet the requirements in doing the will of God. The word revolution does not denote violence in a positive state of mind but is used by negative forces to instigate it. Revolution denotes motion, we were indoctrinated by the system at an early stage in life in a negative motion.

Think positive always and be optimistic in your anticipations as things and circumstances are not as bad as it may seem. it's better to be a live dog than a dead lion. Always be thinking of the luxury of it all. Indulge in positive thoughts and make time to meditate. Sing love songs in the shower and if not aloud hum them. Try to interact with nature, look at the clouds regardless of the color if it's blue and white the sun will shine and if it's grey there is moisture in the making.

Listen to the birds chirp melodies to soothe your mind, feel the wind blow and watch the tree branches sway, see flowers blooming on the horizon and the honey bees feasting on blossoms to soothe your mind. I can just imagine you saying to yourself all that sounds good but who have time for that? You must make the time because you owe it to yourself. There are people that depart this life prematurely without living to enjoy it, When you get to that point it's time to cut the losses pick up your back pack and relocate mentally.

Life was made for living and regardless of the circumstances we encounter, life still goes on it's not over until it's over and the old lady sings. There is no need for you to spend the time you have all stressed out in the process of survival before your appointment with death comes. As I grew up to maturity on my island I always seek to have the association with an older male friend and found it beneficial. I listened to their advices and by them sharing their experiences it helped me to make the right choices.

The reality of it all is to be aware of the components of our spiritual being, the ultimate is our soul that is rarely mentioned but is the most valuable asset we possess. I came across a gesture that states that one man's fear is another man's fortune meaning what is good for the goose is not necessarily good for the gander. The question is what does it profit a man to gain the whole world with all its riches and loose his soul.

We should protect ourselves from excessive rays of the sun and insist on mediating in the moonlight. Layup spiritual treasures by sowing seeds of compassion to fulfill needs. Enjoy the pleasures of material luxuries but do not worship them, always make time to give thanks to the source of our being. Life is a process and all processes require a source to produce products and waste. Always allow our mentality to produce productive thoughts.

With adequate eloquence and persistence I anticipate achieving my goal of accessing the minds of humanity in the process of salutatory restoration of sanity. The spoken word is both potent and dangerous, the words we utter disclose the substance in our thoughts. A mind is a terrible thing to waste and our spoken words can be sharper than a two edges sword and the danger of it all is once it's uttered it cannot be retracted. In situations where a decision must be made to achieve the correct end product, it's best to have it pondered by our hearts.

A soft verbal response turns away harshness but bad words can stir up anger, we can be at peace with ourselves and enjoy our lives as it was meant to be. All the people that are ignorant of the facts regardless of their material substance, they will eventually perish. It's best to avoid loud and abnoxious people, as long as we pursue the right pathway there is a bright future beyond the tunnel. Our responsibility is to take charge and direct the compass of our life in the right direction.

Life is not a bed of roses, there are ups and downs and many curves and it does not work on automatic, it has to be monitored and directed on a progressive agenda. Always be in total control at all times as there will be times when we will encounter obstacles. If you are observant you will see that the two most utilized words in this venture are changes and actions, that's what it's all about here. All that I have discovered in my researches I'm sharing here with you all, you do have the right to do your own research to validate the facts.

Bearing in mind that there's only one truth, all things in the universe were created, we were made by a decision made in a conference by God in three dimensions. The preceding disclosures are facts of reality for you to deal with, this case is closed but can be reopened with permission. I'm proud to declare that I am a child of the true and living Almighty God in three dimensions JC&H, a sheep of his pasture and an instrument to be utilize for his purpose.

Christ is Lord and on him as the solid rock I am secured by Holy the Spirit, all other ground is sinking sand. Although there are other forces in competition for the acquisition of my soul, it is well with my soul in the hands of the Lord. Being a fruit of my mother's womb, I'm blessed and washed in the blood of Jesus for the remission of my sins both inherited and committed.

There are acts of God and acts of nature with all its contents is the most intricate aspect of creation, think for a moment let's consider all the massive oceans, rivers, ponds and streams of water. Over centuries and to this moment in time there have been no report of any leakage of water from this planet earth to interrupt any of the other planets, that's truly amazing. I will now declare that the happiness in our lives rely on the blossoms in our hearts, most mortals rely on acquiring material things to make them happy.

Never rely on anyone to make you happy regardless of what they have to offer, that is a gross error, always seek ways to show appreciation to the source of our existence. Don't be selfish in your doings but stay in full control, do what's best to survive as life is what you make it. Ignorance is caused by lack of knowledge and the ignorant ones among us are up for grabs by the negative forces.

I recently discovered three new religions and in a short period of time they are loaded with participants, because no matter what comes along regardless of their ideology there are vulnerable people out there. They will be eventually be consumed by them because of ignorance caused by lack of knowledge. It's inconsequential to debate the things of God and I insist on not getting involved in any, occasionally I am confronted based on my beliefs that I try to share with people.

We all will encounter from time to time certain circumstances in this life and most circumstances eventually work themselves out over time. We are involved in the system of material things, but try not to indulge in the stress industry as it's taking over people's minds. In most cases mainly because they try to live above their means. The heaviest mental load to carry is a grudge against someone, regardless of what is involved try not to hate anyone as long as you keep your safety armor on.

If at any time you and someone do not get along for any reason it's time to migrate out of their space, this is a fact, as I have had problems with the evil adversary whereby I had to remind him that I'm a possession of God. This world consist of all kinds of people, there is good, bad and indifferent people that enjoy making other people's lives miserable. When we go to bed to rest at nights always give thanks to our sustainer of life, press the delete button and have a good night rest enjoying sweet dreams.

There will be a new day dawning in the morning, whatever situations we encounter we must call on the Lord for help when we need it. Our lives are on a obstacle course so it's beneficial to be alert at all times. Always make your gestures positive and potent like a bank deposit, we must not make commitments we cannot keep. Dreams are desires, and are for real do not give up on them, if you desire them to come through do not oversleep. In this life it is necessary to set goals and consistently work towards achieving them.

Never give up on any of your aspirations by inducing a lack of courage, it is essential that we commence the process in order to achieve our goals. The following is a song I wrote and is seeking someone to put it in motion enhanced by musical instrument.

Life sure seem like a gabble
Love is not a toy
The best attitude is to be meek and humble
We must make decisions to create joy
Without rain from the skies the earth is tough
Perseverance of circumstances will prevail
Endurance is the key to conquer
Cast out our chain of abilities and we will anchor
As we pursue life's journey
We must honor and acknowledge the source
Let us jump the hurdles we encounter
We must do our best to stay the course

Life is too short to live with regrets so live and love every one that we encounter and avoid the ones that are intolerable, everything that transpires is for a reason. I am convinced that every human life has a blue print like the ones done by architects for a house. There is a drawing that specifies the pathway each of us have to travel. There will be times when we have to take time out to allow the winds of the challenges we encounter to blow by.

There will incidents when we get caught up contemplating who is right and who is wrong and get confused as to what's right or wrong. Of all the attires that we wear our presentation including our utterances and demeanor declare our true identity. A bad attitude is a recipe for resentment from others, the four pillars that this system of things sit on are credit, deception, fraud and greed. Always be careful and alert of the words free, win and scam.

Always be careful of the people that we associate with there are people out there who are like wolves in sheep clothing, in the mix that pretend to be friends. A friend should be someone that we can confide in and trust with our lives without motives unconditionally. Although there is a freedom of speech under the first amendment what we say can at times be detrimental based on executive orders. The acting friend that is dangerous is the one that say something you said that you didn't.

Our tears are liquidated substances of our emotions, always be careful not to get submerged in them as there will be circumstance's to endure.

There are tears of sadness if being hurt both mentally and physically, and tears of joy caused by happiness, joy, satisfaction and laughter. Our mental sensitivity is an essential aspect of our being and allow us to achieve and enjoy the pleasures of our lives. In the pursuit of life we encounter enormous amount of experiences, vital information and practical necessities.

There is an art of dealing with each of them individually and effectively whereby instead of suffering the consequences negatively we achieve satisfaction. That's why I will continue to reiterate the importance to acquire vital information from potent literature so as not to become vulnerable. The two most popular means of being deceived are religions and the monstrous system of things. They both are devised and implemented industries to benefit the evil adversary, always be alert.

I've been recently informed that the disease known as cancer is not a disease but a business to generate monetary substance to elevate the system of things. The supposedly health care industry is fueled by human mechanics known as doctors who make diagnosis to fertilize the drug/medication industry. The drug industry parasitically acquire enormous amount of finance and in return compensate the doctors.

Happiness is a state of the mental heart that nourishes our state of mind, there are times when a piece of mind elevate us to a higher altitude than the whole. In most cases it's essential to do adjustments to our mental paradigms to achieve the desires of our heart. We are all on a train called life whereby there is a track to travel on, stations to stop so people can hop on and hop off. Among them will be family, false and real friends, associates of all kinds as it take all kinds of people to make this world.

SYMPTOMS OF LOVE.

Generosity, compassion, Emotions, Satisfaction.
Happiness, Positivity, Authenticity, Reliability.
Sanctity, Sanity, Transparency, Honesty, Truth.
Affection, comfort, passion, Meekness, Tenderness.
Caring, Sharing and Joy.

Love is the answer, never allow your being to operate outside the realm of moderation, there were people that exited this life prematurely before living it due to abusive indulgences. It's of vital importance at an early stage of life to seek and choose a career or some form of means to acquire monetary substance for sustenance. Do not allow life to become stagnant, vacations are healthy in order to get to know various other places and people.

The color white is a neutral pigment that can be manipulated to derive any other color except black, the only color that can be derived from black is light black when white is induced. There are no white humans in this entire world, they may be lightly colored but that's not white. Humans have been indoctrinated otherwise whereby the color white is being promoted as superior. Regardless of our color we all were made to be equal regardless of our origin, color or creed.

Vulnerability existed since Eve as she allowed herself to be deceived to disobey God and bore two children for Lucifer, also there were evidences of incest in the process. Until this day there are descendants of Lucifer among us all murderers, atheists and other evil doers but their days are numbered. God hates sin but we all have sinned and come short of the glory of God, the good thing is that we are given the opportunity to pray for forgiveness, cleansing and pardon to derive remission of them.

A human's beauty is in the head and can be exhibited in our demeanor, it's better to be our real selves than to be discovered to be someone else. Here I am again reminding you my readers to seek and acquire another of my book "Visions for our Mission" by Noel Grace @ Amazon.com, Barnes and Nobles and Xlibris.com.

I will advise you to take some time out and do an assessment of life, I guarantee that you'll be amazed at the enormous faculties intact in the process. There have been several times in my moments of seclusion that I found myself overwhelmed with technicalities. There are laws, rules and regulations to abide by, laws of God, laws of man, laws of nature and others. We all as humans tend to violate them at times to achieve certain goals, some defaults can be overlooked while others we are required to pay penalties for.

Whatever the outcome it all boils down to the choices and decisions we made in the pursuit, it's of vital importance that we exercise contemplations and ponder the eminence. In most cases there are alternatives whereby time is of the essence, be sure you do not find yourself at the wrong place at the wrong time. Good and genuine friends are difficult to come by and when you find one that you confide in there is a tendency to share your experiences with them.

This is detrimental as it's best not to become a casualty of your own utterances, as there are times when portions are added or subtracted to convey the wrong message. Hypocrites and parasites are always hovering around to indulge in the equation to cause problems, it's beneficial to watch your steps on the route.

Here we go again, our God is an awesome God in three dimensions, he is precisely systematic and function in sequence. Humanity is at the mercy of God, Jesus the only begotten son of the father and the inferior evil adversary. The two main priorities are the expansion of God's kingdom on this planet earth as it is on planet heaven. Second in the sequence is the acquisition of our souls, the most valuable commodity.

Due to the goodness and mercy of God, humanity was given the privilege of choice. Eternal paradise on the new earth when the fire goes out and it cools off or in the lake of fire with the evil adversary. My advice to you is to seek now the Lord while he still can be found, call upon him while he's near to acquire refuge in him.

Happiness is generated by the peace of our mental faculties not a luxury, it's a piece of mind not a whole. Material things and financial resources cannot nourish happiness, it can only suffice it. Life itself is a luxury as it was given to us as a gift with ribbons of blessings and mercy on it, and can be perpetuated if not abused. I am convinced that human life is predestined as we all have an appointment with death at different times.

I will now appeal to the worldwide humanity population to wake up from their slumber and smell the flavor of the realities of life. Be not selfish in your doings as sharing is caring and there are compensation packages that awaits us based on our deeds. Always cast bread on the waters of life with compassion and some day it will greet you with attributes of blessings.

The Electronic Transmission System

T he electronic transmission system named the world wide web was developed decades ago and is also called the net or internet, I cannot see us humans in existence without it. The efficiency of it all have proven that without it civilization would have been like an automotive running out of fuel. One of the most essential area is communication by telephones. I will admit that I'm addicted to it as I spend a large percentage of my time on it both day and night.

There is an area called social media whereby we have the privilege to interact with other people around the entire globe. Yesterday I was amazed to be talking to a female on the continent of Australia and after to someone on the African continent. Presently we are in the year 2020 and approximately 100 years ago in primitive times there were huge communication companies that owned infrastructures that ran lines on poles along streets and bi-ways connecting both businesses and residential customers to be able to communicate.

Here in the US I can remember one company named Ma-Bell that had a huge fleet of vans with equipment to maintain and service their system by technicians. That large company was abolished after being consumed by another monster. All of the preceding information that I disclosed have been abolished because we are using wireless cellular phones that have the capability to do all that and beyond. I have an office that was transferred here to my home when I sold my business with a desktop PC and sometimes for weeks is not turned on.

I am able to do everything on my cellular phone wireless, there is a new system developed by technology called blue tooth whereby information can be transferred from one equipment to another without any interaction. It is truly amazing that all that information is travelling in the atmosphere with no interceptions, interactions or disturbances. There are several companies competing to acquire customers based on pricing for service.

I originated from the island of Jamaica in the West Indies and own some land there that I inherited from my parents, it's mountainous there and I have been contacted by companies there that's asking me to rent then a location. Their motive is to acquire high altitudes to place an antenna to transmit media. There are worldwide locations with satellites effectively transmitting substance internationally and I've never heard of any outage in any area of that systems.

I am an author and have the capability to store and accumulate enormous amount of documentations in my cellular phone and when it is full I am able to transfer it to a pin drive. I am convinced that technology is one of the best viruses humanity have contracted. Based on the impact it have on civilization it's a positive achievement, I'm making sure the i-pads are not omitted from this equation, it's been utilized to do marvellous things.

There should be a book out there to cover it all, if not that's a project for a qualified author. I wish I had that opportunity but here I am working on this book in the effort of advertising the realities of life. The responsibility of an author is not a simple one, it's a major challenge that sometime at nights we lose sleep as substance come to our intellect and we have to get up to document or lose them. I have been resenting watching the television for quite a while as it distracts my mind, I'm able to acquire vital information through the internet on my phone.

On line is the term used for utilizing the internet to acquire just about anything, presently we are able to do any kind of transactions using our phones. The main source of payment is the use of credit and debit cards and due to the possibilities of interceptions during the transactions its becoming very risky. Recently I learned of a lady that drove up to a drive through at a fast food store that gave the attendant her credit card, she observed him taking pictures of it with his cellular phone.

That lady parked her car and called the police, when they came she pointed him out and they took his cell-phone and there was several pictures of credit cards in it. The only safety for protection is that there's a number on the rear of the card that's required to complete all transactions, all he had to do was picture both sides. We are living in a time when acts of fraud are so prevalent that it's close to be categorize it as an industry. regardless of the pace of technology development there are individuals that can override any protection codes.

Presently there is a fraudulent multi-million dollar scam industry that's flourishing and there are new ones popping up daily. I was recently approached by a popular one and based on the nature on the solicitation I was required to fill in a form with all my personal information like my s/s # and date of birth. This is a warning to all my readers, do not do it because they will have the opportunity to impersonate you for all the wrong reasons. That was not the first time so what I did was to put a block on all those numbers so there can be no repetition.

As a matter of fact that's useless as all they have to do is call from a different number, it's becoming a battle to survive the pitfalls. Here's how you can discern a crank call, usually you will hear background sounds like a lot of people interacting with various other customers. We can acquire practically anything on line and in some cases have it deliver to our doorstep. The peculiar thing about it all is flexibility and the ability to do business internationally.

Here in the US I know of a monster multi-million dollar business that operate online and have huge warehouses in most major cities with delivery trucks that do both residential and commercial deliveries. The printed media both newspapers and magazines are under attacked by competing with the electronic media as there are sites on the internet to obtain news, information and entertainment just by downloading an app. I can remember back in the primitive era when there were newspaper men that deliver newspapers door to door.

There is a huge reduction in mailing through post offices as by using e-mail addresses instead of practical mailing addresses most mails are delivered electronically with the exception of packages. That means less visits to the mail boxes and less mail men and women, there is also a gross loss in revenue due to the reduction of mailing stamps sales. The package section of that outfit is still in tacked so it's become job security for the mailing staff. I'm privileged to be getting up there in aging as lots of people depart earlier.

I was accustomed to go to the pharmacy to acquire my inventory of medications, I have recently realized that just by downloading an app on the net for that pharmacy I'm able to order refills and also have them delivered. Whenever a new one is prescribed by the doctor it's electronically transmitted to my pharmacy to add to my inventory. As I have disclosed that I'm an author I will inform you that after four months I managed to complete another book and submitted the entire transcript in one file to the publisher, that's amazing.

In this system of things including the new world order devised by the evil adversary. Money is not the source but a resource and fuel, the medias derive riches from investing in indecencies like nudity, fantasy, deceptions, delusions, dishonesty, and faulty conceptions. The victims are human beings who are vulnerable due to lack of essential knowledge. The world wide web is infested with scammers that also advertise and collect money mostly from credit cards, they do not deliver accordingly because they are thieves.

This is a warning, do not store any delicate or personal information in your phone like your date of birth, bank account numbers or s/s number, photos and contacts are fine. The following numbers usually only ring once anticipating your call beck to acquire their requirements don't do it. Here are the following numbers any number beginning with 370, 371, 375, 381, 563, 255, 973 or #90 and #09. The hackers have developed a technology whereby they have the capability to extract data from your phones as all information is stored on the sim card.

There have developed a multi-million dollar industry whereby they target wealthy people who are ignorant of the system and by acquiring their personal information they go on a roll. They have developed a technical system called sim swapping whereby they utilize the information they acquire from people's phones and supply the required information to the phone company. They will request that all the information on the people's sim card be transferred to a new number in their possession.

Whoever their target is whenever they try to use their phone they will be informed that their phone service is disconnected. During the investigation for the restoration, the time that transpired to get their service back the scammer being in full control empty out the bank accounts of their targets and transfer millions of dollars electronically to their improvised accounts. Some experts in California developed a technology to track down scammers and began with the high end ones. They identified one in NY city living a lavish lifestyle residing in an expensive high rise in Manhattan, he was accosted.

That guy was driving very expensive cars travelling in private jet planes and partying wild, the police got involved and captured him. He appeared in court for the first time accompanied by an expensive attorney and pleaded not guilty. There were some victims of the scam system present in court and the total sum stolen exceeded five million dollars based on those in attendance. We are in serious trouble, in the case of credit cards someone need to develop a censor that can scan the chip on them to send the information to the seller on the other end.

It is absolutely dangerous to verbalize that information on the cards on the versatile internet. I hope there is someone in this audience that can instigate the development of that technology and send them to all credit card holders. For goodness sake it would seen that we are being overtaken by fraudulent gangsters. Although this may seem irrelevant in this dialogue with my audience, I will disclose that I resent getting involved in any debates or controversies.

I much prefer utilize my time meditating and personally communicate with my maker and sustainer. Here we go back on track, here is another industry I will elaborate on it's the massive financial establishments. This area of resource management requires a enormous amount of confidentiality as it's a prime target for fraudulent transactions and expensive inconsistencies. This industry consist of numerous institutions called banks which are the main secured storage for cash.

Most of the transactions are done electronically, credit and debit cards are issued by banks for the circulation and distribution of funds. Someone must have an history of a good credit rating to acquire credit cards from banks, debit cards are the opposite as we are permitted to utilize them as a tool to spend our own money to pay for purchases and bills. The system have been abused whereby the less fortunate ones among us try to live above their means by using credit cards. The preceding declaration causes chaos on the system to be more stringent on allowing such malpractices.

Gone are the days when we could manipulate our access to acquire and utilize our money. Distribution is another way that can be utilizes to access the electronic systems, one of the popular source is called ATM located at public locations to do financial transactions. It's somewhat unsafe as thieves have the privilege to intercept if there is a lack of security. We still have the privilege to write or receive checks and acquire cash from them with proper identifications. Most bills especially utility ones are being payed electronically.

The down side of that is if there is a deficiency like lack of funds and that bill is payed the bank in most cases charge a $35 fee, that can be override. It's highly beneficial to live our lives in moderation and maintain a good credit rating, as by doing so we have the privilege of acquiring mortgage loans to get homes and live a decent life and also get car loans to drive decent cars. At the end of the day it all boils down to our capability to exercise self-control to be eligible for all the opportunities that comes along.

There are three things that comes not back, spoken words, a speed arrow and neglected opportunities. The next system I will elaborate on is mobility, I came from my island of origin to reside in the USA forty years ago and when I got here the major ground means of transportation were railroad trains, busses and taxicabs. The first one attacked and destroyed totally by the electronic system was the taxicab industry. At that time all major cities were infested by taxicabs.

Rarely did we had to call them all we had to do was to get to the street and look for one without the occupance light on and wave our hand. Presently it's now the year 2020 and there are numerous sources to facilitate our transportation needs, I did a research of the one I use most and discovered that they are comprised of more than seven million units worldwide. All we have to do is download the app for the one we choose and we can choose more than one also, and there are drivers that service more than one company.

The intricate thing about the system is that when you download the app there is a form to fill in with your credit or debit card information on it. Here we go again it's like we are trapped in a web but the key element of the service is convenience, we call to inform them as to our destination and when they come and we get there we only say thanks. There are lots of people that own cars no more so they don't have to pay for insurance and maintenance of them.

No problem with parking we have the opportunity to relate to the drivers as we ride along and at times get some important information. One driver told me that their percentage of the cost for the trips is lodged automatically to their account in their banks. Of course we still have the busses, both the city owned ones and private ones for trips, excursions and there are some very expensive ones. Recently I had the opportunity to converse with an airplane mechanic.

I was informed that most jet planes are equipped with a self-control system whereby each trip is preprogrammed in the computer and the only time the pilot intervene is for taking offs and landings. They are able to override it, but that's amazing so they are just accompanying it just in case. I will interject one of my favorite systems, it's called the GPS it's truly amazing that with all the millions of cars on the hi-ways and bi-ways this system function effectively without any intrusion or interceptions.

Firstly the transport system that I use for my mobility is operated by the use of the GPS and in most cases using cell-phones or dash screens. The system operates efficiently and precise on locating the targeted locations with turn by turn instructions. Most of the new cars have it built into its electronic system with a screen on the dashboard. Technology is the order of the day and it keeps getting more prominent by the day.

I no longer use a key to open my front door as it only require a sensor that's on my key ring. Due to the nature of my illness I'm being monitored by a company that's several states away, all I have to do is enter all the required statistics in a I-pod press the submit button and off it goes in seconds. My son lives in Saudi Arabia and I'm able to interact with him on my phone in a video format whereby we see each other.

As I disclosed to you that I'm an islander, on a regular phone call we are charged by the minute and sometimes we talk for long periods without realizing the financial consequence until the bill is sent to me by e-mail. Now there exist a social media app that we can do calls worldwide both regular and videos at no extra cost as long as the other party have that downloaded on their end also.

Based on your participation in this dialogue I anticipate that you don't mind me sharing my experiences with you on this subject. There exists a large nationwide distributor of vital commodities in the USA and my favorite place to shop. This morning I got a vibrant message on messenger with its emblem intacted to congratulate me by stating that I'm a winner of a $1,000 gift card. Based on my experiences on this internet fraud industry I requested them to keep it.

The preceding disclosure is to make you be aware of what's out there so you do not get caught in the mud lake of deceptions called scams. On my way to a predestined location, I initiated a conversation with my driver by complementing him about the tranquility of his car ride. He responded by disclosing to me that the car is a hybrid, meaning it operates on dual power and at that moment it was propelled on batteries.

In this age of electronic transmission most of the new car manufacturers are utilizing this new technology, whereby some cars consist of an engine and an oversized battery. Whenever the engine runs it does two things propel the car and charge the battery, the driver have the capability to choose what they need to drive on. When it's running on batteries it's very quiet but each charge only last for a while.

I will always insist in not getting involved into any debates or controversies as I'm entitled to my views and opinions, no one is compelled to agree with them. I pledge to serve the Lord with gladness for he is good and his mercy endures everlasting. I discerned early in my life that the Lord was with me, I came out of my mother's womb to life in tears but knew that I'd be one of his chosen. Let us all come to realize how good he is and that his mercy endures forever, father we give you thanks and praise.

To God be the glory and I made the commitment to praise him to my last breath.

Based on my observations and discernment of trends and momentums I see civilization heading in a direction where humanity will encounter difficulties in not far a distant in existence. At this point in time 2020 I'm calling on all the scientists to visualize beyond the mountain to discern the dangers waiting for us up ahead and devise means to counteract and divert the trends of the present in order to rescue humanity. I must say the directives issued in the holy history book reveal that was not the way God had planned it.

The important aspect of it all is that there is the electronic transmission system available to issue directives worldwide. Over time various religions have issued scare warnings that Jesus is coming soon, and cause people to put up barricades like there's a hurricane on the horizon. The fact of the matter is that he is Omni presently already here doing the will of the father and working in one accord with Christ.

The end of time is nowhere in sight as there are other generations to come after us, the good book denotes that a thousand years in the sight of God is like an evening gone. The tribulation period alone is a thousand years and there will come times when there will be wars and rumors of wars and eventually the battle of Armageddon. The good thing is that we all have a destination based on our choices and God rules our destiny.

Systems Within The System

The four primary pillars that the American system sit on and exist are credit, deception, fraud and greed and we become food for it. We must learn to beat it at its games in order to be a victor and not a victim, the average ones among us suffer because of ignorance. The term American dream is a myth created by the system to pull us in so that we can be controlled and manipulated by it. Most of the institutions and the monster called cooperate are positioned to take disadvantage of the masses.

They pay big money as bribe to the officials that we choose by voting them in to represent and protect us to maintain the status-quo. It's about time we all wake up and smell the roses in order for us not to be manipulated by contributing to the defaults of this system. Technically when we ignore the procedures we become just players meaning preys, and the beat goes on. It is essential to be cautious of the folks we associate with, not everyone we know is qualified for that privilege of being a friend, and most of them are just acquaintances.

A friend should be someone we can confide in and trust with our life without motives, unconditionally. Always be careful of what we utter as a spoken word can be a gem or a sword, yes we are protected by the freedom of speech act under the first amendment. Notwithstanding whatever we say can be detrimental based on executive orders. The words silent and listen are relevant as they are spelt with the same letters. There are times that you'll find yourself in a state of curiosity, only facts can cure that symptom.

Listen more and speak less, always allow the talkers to exhaust their contents ask for more then send them on to the next victim. Be sure not to underestimate the issues I raised in the contents of this publication as it's meant to be substantial enough to awake you from your slumber. At all times be subjected to the laws of the land, get involved with nature and keep up with technology because that's the direction everything is going in. There are times that I contemplate how did the generations before us existed without the computer with the internet.

Back when I was a child I was very curious and asked a lot of questions, one day I observed a tree growing on top of another, I questioned that incident and asked for a clarification of the act and discovered that the new one is called a parasite. I was also informed that there are incidents when that parasite gets large enough to choke the original tree and kill it. As I grew older I realized that parasites are not necessarily a robber but they seek ways to suffice their existence.

The time of maturity started setting in on me and I then realized that there are human parasites also and that became scary to me. Every human was given enough potentials to survive for the duration of our lives, but there are people that do not devote enough time to identify it and utilize their potentials to live and enjoy life rather than just existing. There have been times when people encounter red tapes, just keep on trying and if you fail try again there are always alternatives.

When I became a teenager there was a guy I knew from a well to do family, we used to play ball and he did well in school and he was eventually sent to a reputable and expensive collage. I didn't see him for a long period of time as we had relocated to a different neighborhood. After years had passed one day I decided to stop by to say hi to his parents and enquire about him. It was in the summer time and I asked his mother for him, she said he is fine and is out back sitting by the pool.

I went to see him and we started reminiscing on the past and he offered me a beer of course I said thanks but no thanks as I do not consume alcohol. Now that we are adults we could relate so I told him about my life being a husband and father of two kids. He also disclosed his achievements, one of them was that he graduated collage with a degree in psychology but does not work as his parents are getting very old, he decided to stay home to take care of them, and I was amazed.

On my side of the coin I was working forty hours a week to maintain my family. On his side it would seem very considerate but to me my stomach got upset as I contemplated that for all those years of schooling and the expenses incurred will go to waste on an old parent's caretaker. There are circumstances when we can consider ourselves as making a sacrifice by tolerating uncomfortable situations. Case in point I have known of abusive situations where married couples remain together for the children's sake, listen to me it's not worth it.

There will become a time when the kids become mature enough to leave the nest and by then it's much too late to recuperate from the pains that you bore both physically and mentally for the duration. I am not aware of your situation or state of mind but I will caution you that civilization is heading in a direction to cause controversy and hopelessness. To suffice existence it's essential to be productive by utilizing and keeping up with technology.

The political system is corrupted as the representatives we voted in are bribed to take positions to propel it and that's not in the interest of us the people. There are bureaucracies in place to protect the system by perpetuating its existence based on greed for currency. There is Wall Street and Main Street two totally different entities and they try to deceive us otherwise. The investment sector and the stock market are on one side of the spectrum and the other side is the banking industry.

They are related based on the shuffling of paper works and commit incest without being accosted for their fraudulent actions. It does not matter what reforms are devised, nothing will change as the people in control of the currency will not allow it and the politicians are in on it deep. Over recent years things have changed so now John Public are aware of the defaults, thanks to C-Span. Although the internet have been used, misused and abused it's still one of the best thing man have invented.

It's more beneficial to be an initiator than an emulator as the human brain have no limit to its potentials. Never be comfortable in any circumstance, always appreciate what you achieved and possess. Keep your eyes and mind open to identify and utilize any opportunity that comes your way. It's amazing the things we can creatively and legally do to beat the system at its games. In the process of identifying it and utilizing the means we can evade moments of stress.

It's a proven fact that females are better handlers of money than men, case in point. I heard the story of a middle aged male that met a much younger female and fell in love with her at first sight, of course love is usually blind. The male in question's father was terminally ill and he had the opportunity to inherit a large fortune. After the passing of his father, being excited about his new lover he communicated that information to her and of course. That caused the relationship to flourish.

Based on her plans she permitted him to having premature intimacy before he left on a business trip. What transpired during his absence was as follows, she managed to have met that dying father. One day while her date was out of town she arranged with a friend of hers who was a pastor so he met her there and performed a marriage ceremony making her the hair of the estate. In my business book that was a creative investment as the son is now secondary on the possession of that estate, sooner or later he'll be informed.

Presently there are many people in existence that possess enormous amount of potentials that they are not aware of and unless they are up to date it's all dormant. Once they are made aware of them they can be activated to be utilized to their benefit and advantage. Imaginations can generate innovations that can be created and packaged to cause visual attractions in order to be rewarded. This will be a constructive criticism that will benefit mental faculties in a magnitude of proportions.

Business is basically a number cavity and is only successful in a volume format, meaning the more you put in is the more you get out of it. The main components of a business are source, products and waste, in the middle of it all is labor. In my personal experience I've sacrificed myself unknowingly for the purpose of elevating people who are involved and I have been used and abused in the name of generosity. I'm consciously aware that the negative spiritual forces are involved and will not ignore it but resist it for survival.

Self-control is essential and plays an important role in this process of the reforming of our minds. Check this out, one day I had the appetite for fish and went to a restaurant to make an order, when the package and the bill came I realized I did not have enough cash on me to pay it. The American way is to immediately reach for the credit card but I'm reformed so I ask the attendant to take it back and reduce the quantity to match the amount of cash I had.

In no time I was on my merry way with no credit card bill to anticipate getting in the mail, these are some of the situations we encounter at times in this system. Cooperate is very tricky, brand name recognition and attractive presentations attract eyes of potential customers. At all times when you go shopping, buy the things that you need and not what attract the eyes to want. Don't get me wrong now, for convenience you do need a card in that case use a debit card whereby you only can use your own money.

Here I am instigating a reform to benefit us rather than the system, start reforming your lifestyle and remember there are times called rainy days. It's of vital importance that there's always a portion of your resources stocked away behind closed doors in the bank. I'm sitting here and can imagine hearing you say, give me a break, are you living in this modern world? Yes I am. Although what I'm trying to instill in you it's possible, it depends on how deep you are in the system.

There is always room for a new beginning, it's never too late for a shower of rain, the fact of the matter is that you need to identify where in the equation you are and is willing to make the necessary changes. There are ways to get your mental faculties synchronized in order to derive the ability to adjust your chain of thoughts. If you own an expensive car and the check engine light comes on the first thing you would do is take it to the dealer that would hook it up to an analyzer to identify the problem and correct it.

Our human bodies are more expensive than a car, likewise it's time to wake up to get connected to the main computer of our being. God, to get a check-up of our faculties. I will interject the following incidents that happened to me early this morning that's trying to create me to be a new member of the victims of the system. To be a victim it's required of us to possess a degree of vulnerability, whereby we operate in a state of vacuum. At 9am this morning my phone rang and I observed that call originated from New York, I answered and was greeted with a refreshing prelude.

The caller stipulated that in 2014 when I had my business rolling full speed, I had bought some investments. After a period of time they discovered some irregularities and it was shut down by the FTC Federal trade commission, a lawsuit was filed and we the members won. They have tried to contact me for quite some time as my portion of the outcome is in holding in the sum of $450,000. This is the catcher, to initiate the process of acquisition I have to pay $ 2400 now.

This was my response, "this sure smell like a bunch of fresh roses but sound like a scam" and he hanged up. Recently I got a call and it was supposedly from my bank and they stipulated that there have been some irregularities with my personal information on my account. What the caller required was all my personal information over the phone to update my account information. That was when I could see Russia from my house so I said thanks but no thanks case closed.

Do not take any shots offered by any medical institution for any disease because these are assumed viruses experimentally developed in laboratories to inject in us humans, to create resource for the health care system. Every so often they design scares to put people in an absorption mode to accept these shots and they are not cheap but paid for by the insurance companies. Last time I checked they were $ 25 per shot, I need a mathematician to help me 25x 300,000,000 if everyone take them.

There have been incidents when things got out of hand because they developed a shot and sent it to a certain continent where it thrived causing a certain sexual disease that is assumed to be incurable. That virus was developed in a laboratory now it's worldwide and being blamed on a certain sexual orientation. There have been institutions set up and equipped with chemicals all in place to capitalize on this created default in the system.

This is a form of fuel for the system to benefit professions to include nurses, doctors, hospitals and funeral parlors, causing the system to flourish. I always discourage individuals not to get involved in any kind of studies as somewhere in the process you will be required to digest some kind of chemical to enhance it to their benefit. Do not drinks any energy drink regardless of the powerful animal on the label, as they are loaded with stimulants and in most cases have a dependency factor.

A major system in the mix is the multi-million dollar utility industry that includes the Electrical power generation and distribution, the water acquisition, storage and distribution for all the different requirements, sewer for the disposal of waste and the refuse systems. For a major part of my life I've been involved in different aspects of the utility systems. My second job was in the preparation and packaging of a products in the nutrition industry.

I was later involved in the bauxite industry whereby they used red soil to process and made alumina that is eventually smelted to become aluminum. I worked in the water treatment department and my job was to purify water for boilers to produce very high pressure steam to turn turbines, those turbines run generators making electricity. It was basically recycling of water whereby after the process the steam is condensed and stored in large containers.

My next job was to clean sewer lines that conveyed sewage to disposal stations with metal snakes, and other issues in the waste department. I eventually got involved into plumbing and eventually owned my own company and we did it all. The construction industry relies on us plumbers to install the lines in the ground and stick them up before they pour the slabs to build the houses on. When I retired and got ill I sold my company to someone in a popular Spanish community.

It's eminent that you'll encounter insinuations mentioned in this publication that are also mentioned in other of my books, I cannot assume which or any of them you had the privilege of reading. The reason for the repetition is that I was given an assignment to deliver and share a message. There is one thing I can assure you is that you will not see any predictions here as I was not given that authority. I must declare that I'm a servant of the true and living God and he utilizes me for his purpose to do his will.

The preceding was an assignment that I was given to instill in you, let's get back to the systems. At the present moment in time I will assume that you are aware of the impact the new wireless cellular phone system with the capability to access the powerful internet plays in our existence. As I sat by my bedroom window this morning, I could see numerous children go by to get on the bus and the alarming thing was that all of them were looking at the screen of a cell-phone.

I consider that degrading to their brains and cause a lack in comprehension of what they are taught at school, I will again reiterate that certain situations are going in the wrong direction. It's never too late for a shower of rain and I will encourage the authorities to get a hold on this dangerous situation, to pave a pathway of progression for the next generation. Do not be deceiver by religions that the end is near, there are other generations preparing to replace us.

The aeronautic system was designed and implemented basically for transporting humanity across the globe name earth. Connecting all nations, color and creed, that created human mobility for migration. Recently the head administrator of the USA government disclosed his objection to any influx of migrants regardless of their origin. On the opposite side of the coin the president of Canada announced his anticipation of his country achieving migrants in millions in the next two years.

Based on the process of productivity and progress, it's been a known fact that immigration is healthy for industrial growth. Although I might have mentioned this before I will again disclose that I originate from a Caribbean island and worked in several industries over years in this country the USA. Based on the curiosity of the possibility of mortal existence on other planets, they sent astronauts in space ships to the moon and concluded that there's none out there.

Guidance for Our Existence

The implications here are guidance for our being for its duration, it's vital and should be made known. In the process of ageing our capabilities including our memory deteriorates, in most cases it requires repetition as an adhesive to attach it to our minds. Penetrate and indulge in the following documentations.

1. The success of our lives relies on the quality of our thoughts, it's imperative to invest in the coordination of our mental faculties.
2. Life is °an important privilege with an allotted amount of time to fulfil a mission, seek to locate imperative visions.
3. Live, love and contribute to needs to be blessed, the compensation package is alive and well.
4. Our value is not determined by our material possessions, but by our deeds, commence the laying up of treasures to be compensated in the future.
5. it's pleasurable to indulge in meditation with our maker, enhanced in the background with sounds of nature.
6. The realization of our mental consciousness generates aspirations to pursue and acquire a successful outcome.
7. it's productive to indulge in mind farming as it creates innovations for producing essential requirements for our existence.
8. Always respect the utterances, views and opinions of others even if you disagree, do not expect them to respect yours.
9. To ignore is a choice but to be ignorant is a defect, seek wisdom from knowledge as its kinetic energy with power and might and enhanced by holy.

10. Each human's life is enhanced by a thought process and God rules our destiny. Take whatever actions that's necessary keep it in forward not reverse.

11. There sure would be a void in our lives without the challenges we encounter, there is always a light beyond the tunnel.

12. Always try to endure the circumstances we encounter in life to the best of our ability, at the end of the rainbow there will be a pot of gold.

13. When night's fall it's time to put our faculties to rest and recuperate in anticipate the dawning of a brand new day with all its blessings.

14. it's of vital importance to synchronize our being with time for accurate functioning, there is a time and place for everything

15. Always differentiate our wants from our needs as our needs are essential for our survival, while wants are fueled by desires.

16. We are all three dimensional, and in conference God in three dimensions but individual in functions decided to make us in his characteristically likeness.

17. If for any reason you allow ignorance to supersede knowledge a vacuum called vulnerability is created to accept and accommodate negativity.

18. Surprises sure make life exciting, do not rely on anyone to surprise you. It's beneficial to invest in yourself within your means.

19. Stress is a byproduct of defective decisions, by investing in stress makes it possible to prematurely exit this life on the stress express.

20. 20. The term world is the total count of humanity, the planet earth is a domain we occupy for a duration of time.

21. It's pleasurable and rewarding to make the right choices and be successful, the secret of survival is not to be selfish seek mean to satisfy needs.

22. Sow good seeds of compassion and some day in the future you will reap the fruits of your labor, as your labor was not in vein.

23. Because humans have devised systems to recreate our mentality in a negative mode to support them, it's important to identify and resent it.

24. Let's all cherish the dawning of each new day and give gratitute to the sustainer of our lives, as there's no gaurantee of us seing tomorrow.

25. Always keep our concentrations focused on the good things in life and anticipate elevating to higher altitudes.

26. Every human being is a self-contained power plant with enormous amount of capabilities to utilize.

27. Always analyze and respect the power of your spoken words before you utter, as once it disburser it cannot be retracted, listen more and talk less.

28. The key to opening the door to abundance is the practice of sharing our prosperity, it's better to give than to receive.

29. it's customary that every human feed their bodies at least three times a day it's of vital importance that we feed our minds with potent nutrients continuously.

30. be sure our affirmations are synchronized with our determinations in order for us to achieve our goals, do not indulge in procrastinations.

31. The negative programming of our minds by the world systems have created a demand for indecency, especially on the internet.

32. The reason why aged males get balled in the middle of their heads is because that's where the antenna is located to supply substance to the brain.

33. The human's will is the most valuable asset we possess as it's the authority that controls our existence, it determines the proper actions to be taken.

34. Common sense enhances the level of our intelligence, adequate wisdom from knowledge is of vital importance in the process of survival.

35. Every human have an appointment with the eminent death at different time and stages, its importance to do what's necessary to enter the next realm.

36. Seek refuge in Christ the Lord to be secured in him and be sure of a place in his house on the new earth named paradise.

37. Don't allow yourself to be deceiver by religions carefully explore the fields before joining the heard, the grass always seem greener on the other side until you get there.

38. Let's all pursue the journey of our lives and explore the realities of our existence, we must be prepared to endure the circumstances for the duration.

39. Color is utilized to determine the difference between good and bad, the darkest color is black and all other colors are derived from it except white. White is not a color or is it pure but a natural pigment that can be manipulated, there are no white humans but some have lightly colored skins.

40. It would be good and pleasant for all us humans to live in peace, love and harmony, it would be like honey to a bee enjoying the sweetness from a fresh bloom.

41. Every human's life is on a blue print with a magnetic force guiding it from inception until extinction, there are situations whereby deception because it be otherwise.

42. None of the contents of these gestures are meant to be instructions, this is an assignment being disbursed for the purpose of encouragement.

43. As long as something is included in our anticipation to be achievable, avoid using the word if instead use when in order to have a positive outcome.

44. There are evidence that the laws of attraction is operating in a reverse mode as the negatives are becoming the norm due to deception from the evil adversity. It's customary for history to repeat itself.

45. 45 Vacuum is created by empowering emptiness, always be careful of our status as our senses operate in a state of vacuum.

46. Cherish whatever you achieved and possess and seek ways to improve it, it's better to have a live mouse than a dead lion.

47. There are no perfections in civilization, vulnerability always complete outcomes and create consequences to endure.

48. Hello world! Always realize that time is similar to fuel, endeavor to utilize it to the maximum before its exhausted and you be at a standstill.

49. We are the world that inhabits this earth, we are all one including animals and vegetation by breathing the same polluted air for our duration of time.

50. It's more expensive to be ignorant than educated, submerged in ignorance we make expensive blunders and have to suffer the consequences.

51. I will declare that material things does not necessarily make someone happy based on my experiences in this life, the true meaning of being

happy is knowing and rely on the source of our existence to supply our needs accordingly.

52. Identify and maintain our stability, never try to emulate others as we possess all the rudiments and capabilities to live and enjoy life to the fullest.

53. it's of vital importance to sow seeds of compassion by seeking to identify and satisfy the needs of the unfortunate ones among us, we'll be compensated.

54. Hope and fear are relevant but not related, loneliness is not a default as it's productive to find someone to confide in.

55. Always maintain an open mind capable of acquiring potent substance, our minds are like parachutes whereby they operate best while open.

56. it's best to insist on crossing the river of consequences and aim for higher altitudes of prosperity overlooking the valleys of distress.

57. Insist on calling people you consider your friends to communicate with them that you thought of them, it's always good to be each others keeper.

58. Although tomorrow is promised to no one always insist on giving thanks to our father, and consider today as being the first day in the rest of your existence.

59. Curtailments retard progress, let freedom reign and may humanity persist in advancing to higher altitudes on this revolving planet earth.

60. If was a song how often would you sing it? The rest room is an ideal venue to practice, I will insist that we all utilize our capabilities and enjoy life to the fullest.

61. Hording is a selfish game while generosity do magnetize our being for compensation in abundance, beyond our imagination.

62. it's beneficial to do a presentation our true self than to be discovered to be someone else, if you are beautiful it comes from your heart.

63. Moments of giving thanks and praise to our maker is essential but our happiness is a vital component of our being, insist on making the best of our possessions.

64. it's possible to commit a negative deed in an instant and suffer the pain and consequences of it for a life time, always insist on doing well.

65. There are always times in this life when circumstances causes pain which it usually does, that does not allow us the right to be cruel always be forgiving,

66. This life is not a game to gamble with as the accurate execution of the power of our will determines the final destination of our soul.

67. As the due on the leaves greet the sunlight of a new day, so should we welcome the privileges we possess and maximize their potentials.

68. it's a tradition that the people that have the most money didn't work to acquire it, they had money work for them.

69. Hope if a doubtful state of anticipation, it's essential to take positive actions to achieve our goals.

70. We are all here on this earth to accomplish a mission and without visions people will perish, seek and acquire the book "Visions for our Mission" by Noel Grace @amazon.com/books and Xlibris.com.

71. The progress of any nation depends on the choices of its people, may we all unite and maintain the gold standard.

72. The compensation system is alive and well, always be alert to be able to identify our blessings to claim them as sometimes they come disguised.

73. The sun does not come up nor the moon go down, the planet earth that we inhabit revolves around them.

74. Always be conscious of the indoctrinations in diversion from the truth and guard our minds from them, it's beneficial to our being.

75. The state of total tranquility called peace is a state of mind and is a preservative for our hearts.

76. Liquid is a state in existence never allow our being to become stagnant, seek ways to motivate and perpetuate it.

77. We all are components of a society and our participation in it cultivates substantial amount of substance to benefit us all.

78. The present trends, pace and development of technology is beneficial to our existence, be sure to get on board and not left behind.

79. There are only two words in the English language that have all five vowels in order "abstemious" and "facetious", please don't ask me for their meaning.

80. Currency is the life and blood of commerce, it's beneficial to devise legal means to acquire, utilize and retain it in abundance.

81. Insist on living a life of purpose with all our faculties in a positive and sequential mode, in order to place an impact on our society.

82. When all is said and done, it's conclusive that life is a predestined venture although it's possible to be at the wrong place at the right time.

83. Although vulnerability is discerned as a negative state of the art, we should always make our intellect accessible for inspirations from our maker.

84. We are the world consisting of mortal inhabitants in a package with a timer on it existing on this planet earth, Our souls have the capability of existing forever on a cleansed earth called paradise by making the right decision.

85. The English language have twenty six letters and this sentence contain them all," The quick brown fox jumps over the lazy dog". Case closed.

86. The challenges in our life's pursuit sometimes are severe to the point of retarding the true purpose of living life to the fullest, still thank God for life.

87. We should not practice being selfish and always keep a song in our hearts, not the one that says..." I am myself and no one else".

88. "Dreamt" is the only word in the English language that ends with the letters MT, our dreams are achievable as long as they are not intercepted by the evil forces.

89. The fastest growing belief system on this earth is a wagon going in the wrong direction called Islam, always be on the lookout not to be dissolved.

90. The human conscious minds have the capability to achieve anything it perceive, put it in motion and be compensated from the outcome.

91. The process of repetition is the adhesive by which substance is attached to our memory folder, it's best to do it again to get it right.

92. it's beneficial to position ourselves to be able to fist on the magnificence of nature, enjoying the fragrance of roses and the chirps of the birds on distant horizons conveyed by the wind.

93. Positive thoughts are mental seeds awaiting to be germinated to substantiate existence, we acquire them by way of meditation.

94. By living well and love much indulge in laughter as it's therapy for our souls, make the best of today like there is no tomorrow.

95. The brain in our head is the main command center of our being and is being supplied with substantial amount of information by our senses, be sure to rest for it to recuperate.

96. Our human being is very complicated but coordinated efficiently consisting of two hearts, two minds, five senses and several other organs, all operating in the natural mode.

97. Our conscious mind, spiritual heart and soul all operate in a spiritual mode, this department of our being is monitored by God our maker.

98. All our decisions are made and executed by our conscious mind based on substance derived by the subconscious from our senses, it's beneficial to have our heart ponder them in the process.

99. Circumstances are results of defective decisions made and does alter cases, do not allow other people's consequences to affect your life. Sometimes it's from wrong deeds they committed previously.

100. Always be cautious in the in the advancement of progression, as it's like climbing a ladder to higher heights, it's easier to descend than to ascend.

101. I'm conscious of the intricacies of my language, there are three words in English that can be spelt forward and backward and have the same meaning. They are "Racecar" "Kayak" and" Level ". Excuse me!

102. Typewriter is the longest word that can be spelt by using all its letters from the top line on the keyboard.

103. Literature is the blood of information that's used to fuel knowledge and manufacture wisdom to nurture our intellect.

104. The electronic media is an essential tool in most areas of our modern existence, but reading produces much more nutrients for our minds.

105. Generosity magnetizes our being in the process of compensation, always be on the lookout for destitution and seek means to satisfy the need. The magnitude of the vacuum created measure the quantity of our reward.

106. it's essential to schedule some time out of our daily allotment to meditate in order to generate productive thoughts. We must come to the realization that all things except the elements of nature originated from a thought

107. Marriage is an institution and for it to be successful the participants must be committed and flexible to tolerate situations to comprise. God did not design it to be a misunderstanding between two immature adults.

108. It was predicted that there will come a time when the older folks will dream dreams and the younger ones among us will see visions. It's beneficial to prepare our intellect for those moments and utilize the substance of it all.

109. Yesterday is history and tomorrow is a mystery that is promised to no one, never allow the past to impede the anticipated progress of the future.

110. Our life is a gift that God gave us with a ribbon on it and in return, the good deeds that we do to the needy ones among us is our gift in return to our sustainer.

111. Life is an obstacle course, if at any time of for any reason we fall we should pick ourselves up and head for the finish line with persistence.

112. Patience is a virtue, we should never give up on our dreams and set our anticipations at a high altitude. Always prepare our emotions to accept and tolerate whatever the outcome is, life goes on and there will always be other opportunities.

113. There are no two absolutely identical human beings in civilization even if you were born twins. Every one of us were uniquely made with different characteristics and capabilities to survive for the duration of our lives.

114. Because of the compensation package system there is a factor of inheritance passed down from deeds committed by our ancestors.

115. All things in the universe are possessions of God, the earth is the Lord's and the fullness thereof, case closed.

116. After is said and done it's of paramount importance that we be aware of our significance in existence. We should endeavor to put an impact on civilization instead of wasting our lives.

117. The image we see in the mirror in just a reflection of us, our true identity is in our heads a section of our brain called the heart. Thereby as a man think so is he.

118. it's of vital importance to do an assessment of our mental faculties to determine the degree of its progress, there are times when it's necessary to make adjustments to the rotation of our mind.

119. The farming of our minds is the most lucrative means of generating material substance, find time to do it and share it.

120. Whatever our minds conceive can be achieved by manipulating the paradigms of our mental faculties, go for it.

121. The reality of our existence denotes that there are three realms to encounter based on our decisions before our first death, seek to achieve directives in order to make the right decision.

122. Always do unto others as you would like them to do unto you, be sure you exercise generosity. The good we do today will someday greet us as blessings in enormous proportions.

123. Always be honest in our dealings with others, if in desperation you require a loan to help you out insist on keeping your commitment.

124. Situations do not always transpire the way we plan them due to the possibility of interceptions by the evil forces. Always be conscious of the circumstances and allow it to work itself out.

125. Always set up a foundation to convey the weight of our substance as it's impossible to transport any liquid in a basket made of straws.

126. The formula for growth is in numeric multiplications, be sure to devise a method to generate a magnitude of units and put them in motion.

127. Always be sure that the contents of our utterances are factually potent as we can be held accountable for any inconsistencies in the equation.

128. Having a periodic meeting of minds is a constructive venture as through the process of dialogues we can derive beneficial substance for our existence.

129. it's beneficial to monitor the quality of the contents that we digest in our bodies, it's the potency of our intake that either damage or enrich the outcome.

130. Usually it's easier to get in than it is to get out, our life is on a one way hi-way. Always give our hearts time to ponder the pros and cons before making decisions.

131. Try to avoid complications, uncertainties and divisive situations, if at any time it sounds too good to be true it's time to head for the border.

132. Always be careful of the word free although the good things in life are supposed to be free, the only thing that's free is the air that we breathe and it's polluted.

133. Think positive always and be optimistic in our anticipations, concentrate on the luxury of having a life with the privilege of everlasting life in paradise based on our decision.

134. Continuously allow peace and love to abide in us and always be our brother's keeper. Cast bread on the waters of life and someday we'll find it.

135. Consider the magnificence of nature, the earth as a circular globe in orbit in the universe among numerous other planets. The world consisting of humanity of various nationalities color and creed inhabit it.

136. To venture is an act of progression and the opposite of procrastination, always aspire elevating to a higher altitude.

137. Never permit the projected dark clouds of today to impede the capability of enjoying the brilliance of a brighter tomorrow. Insist on giving thanks to our maker and sustainer continuously.

138. Equip ourselves with an armor of faith, truth and peace with happiness in the pursuit of our being, the battle is not for the swift but for those who can endure to the end.

139. Envision our lives through rose colored mirrors, enhance it with the rays of a brilliant sunny day and acquire enormous prosperity.

140. Always allow our lights to shine with positive words and deeds so others will see our good works, be not selfish in our doings be generous to benefit humanity.

141. I will reinterate that Christ is Lord/Son/Word/Truth and a member of the trinity of God and contineously serve him. The promises of God are sure as long as we do his will and keep his comandments, goodness and mercy will follow us for all the days of our lives.

142. All the preceedings that were disclosed in this survival venture was designed to be similar to a cake. The balance of the contents of this publication to be the icening on it. Let me remind you that life is a gifted previlage and we should enjoy it's pleasures.

143. Now that I have completed my assignment, I anticipate that it will impliment the conscious mental impact intended. Let peace and love abide.

Declaration of Spiritual Facts

It's not my intent as a visionary massenger and mentor to get you involved in deceptions, and whatever implications that are included in this publication it's of vital importance. It's customary to always commence from the beginning but in this venture and the nature of it we will begin before the beginning. There will be some very concequential facts disclosed here so I will instigate your attention, tolerance and request that you utilize your comprehensive skill.

The following is not based on any religious institutions as yours truly is not affiliated with any religion, instead I'm in a relationship with the Father by way of Christ the son and through the power of Holy the Spirit. Here we go..... God is an invisible spirit in three dimensions known as the trinity and existed beyond the realms of glory before the beginning. This trinity consist of Jehovah the father, Christ his Son, Lord, Word, Way and Truth, saving for last is the powerhouse as the ultimate is Holy the Spirit.

A spirit cannot utter, die or document anything in writing the holy history book known as the bible preceded the beginning. Although it contains things and actions of God, it was not written by God or is the word of God. The bible was written and compiled by numerous professionals in different aspect of life and they were inspired by God. The bible contain directives and commands for humanity to comply with in the process of existence. God sees, listens, rewards, compensates, protects, issue instructions and guidance.

Religions were devised and instituted by the evil adversary and designed to place a barrier between us and our maker and sustained. A large percentage of huminity participate in them so religions are in place as an industry and appointed his chosen administrators. He named them pastors, ministers, prophets, priests, missionaries, fortune tellers and others. This a multi-billion dollar industry, the sad part of it is that it takes disadvantage of the most distressed and unfortunate ones among us.

Last time I checked there were those that got so wealthy that they travel on private jet plains. Religions specify their flocks as being christians meaning followers of Christ who is God and a member of the trinity that should promote unity. There is only one true and living God and religions are divisive and teach different doctrines based on their design and beliefs. One thing they all do is try to communicate with the father in the names of Jesus and his mother Mary.

Most religions teach their congregation that in the beginning was Jesus the word, and he was with god and was god. The fact of this matter is that if Jesus was in existence at that time, God would have been a 4nity rather than a 3nity. Jesus was born as a son of man by the Virgin Mary ages after the beginning of time and long after the first water cleansing of this earth. Another issue is the commandments issued from God to us humanity to live by that are being violated in massive proportions.

A name denotes identity with attachments, it have no other significance, I will implicate that a name is not like a key that can open doors to access anywhere neither locations or privileges regardless. Here I am again trying to disclose the truth to set humanity free from bondage to eventually acquire the gift with a red ribbon on it. I will insist on reiterating with my eloquence that Christ is not the surname of Jesus as indicated in the bible. They are two separate spirits coordinated in doing the will of the father.

It was predicted in the scriptures that the word will become flesh and dwell among us as a human. The following was the procedure that transpired, holy the Spirit utilized a small portion of Christ the word and implanted it as a human seed inside the womb of the Virgin Mary. After the pregnancy duration Mary gave birth to a son of man named Jesus so the scripture was fulfilled. Glory to God in the highest not in heaven, may his peace and good will be with us.

Based on my writings in an effort to preserve the mentality of international humanity, I was recently accosted by a minister of a religion instigating a confrontation but I'm not a victim of ignorance. Based on my assignment to spread the truth to all this world I am compelled to resist all attacks from the evil adversary and his agents. I'm not interested to get involved in any controversy, confrontations or debates concerning the things of God.

Today again I was accosted by another pastor that quoted to me some scriptures trying to prove me wrong about the things of God. Christ our God, Lord, Word is Truth and the only way and route to the throne of grace. Religions have failed and it's necessary for people that's participating in them get to know the truth. Although the bible is recognized as the authority, in my research and assessment of its contents there are errors in it that's too numerous to mention.

There's no one to blame as it was not edited and no one owns it's copyright, it was written by several contributors through inspirations, including options and suggestions. God rules our destiny and is the owner of our breath, it's beneficial to give him honor, glory, thanks and praise continuously. Our life is a gift from God if we make it that way, never be a prisoner of your past experiences. It was a lesson and not meant to be a life sentence, to endure and suffer. Life consist of numerous phases there are times when neutrality intervene and it feels like getting to a crossroad.

At moments like those it's compulsory that all our mental components be put in motion to make essential decisions. Who am I to question the things of God, I simply classify myself as being only a visionary messenger, one of my main concern is the privileges the evil adversary possesses. I perceive him as being omnipresent which is dangerous for him to have access to pollute the mental faculties of all humanity. One of my social media associates in Lagos Nigeria on the continent of Africa informed me of his encounter with him there.

He is described as the evil god of this world to be guided by who accept him as such. He had the privilege of going to heaven because that's where he originated, but when Jesus got there two of his priorities were to confiscate his passport so he has no access to pollute the angelic forces and change his name from Lucifer to Satan. I will now bring it to your attention that life is not bed of roses, there are rivers to cross and mountains to climb overlooking the valleys of adversities.

We all as humans enter this life crying as we acquired the privilege of life on a timer, and leave here quietly asleep bound for one of two destinations based on our choices. Earlier in my life I realized that there is a serious decision for me to make, and became aware of my options. I eventually submitted my being to the father by way of Christ and got submerged in the blood of Jesus for the remission of my sins. As Jesus demonstrated in water while being here on this earth as a human.

Today as I sit here in this chair I can proudly disclose my identity as being a child of the only true and living God and a sheep of his pasture with the confidence that my soul is secured in him. Over the years I became aware of the sequence of how the Godhead operates and I will share it with you. God the father is the executive and operates like a mainframe computer in total authority. Secondly holy his Spirit is like the police department enforcing all the laws, regulations and commands with power and might.

Christ the son and Lord is the real deal by doing the total management to please the father. Jesus is a portion of him so he is like his administrator and representative cooperating with him in doing the will of the father in one accord. As it was predicted they are in the process of preparing a place for us called eternal paradise. Based on the doctrine being implanted in the minds of humanity with the false hope of going to heaven, it's apparent that there will be a lot less spirits in paradise than anticipated, only God knows.

At this time in the year 2020 I am appealing to the entire humanity in this world not to allow themselves to be indoctrinated by religions with the false hope of going to heaven or glory. Two days ago I was accosted by a Christian female that instigated that Jesus stated in the bible that he and the father Jehovah the executive of the trinity are one. Ouch, that's major news to me and I hope she will be allowed enough time in her lifetime to acquire mental recuperation. I should have informed her that the father have never been a human.

Here I am as a visionary messenger doing my part in the process of spiritual mental reformation in preparation for our eternal destiny. Do not allow yourself to be deceived by religions, seek and find the right pathway. Let your utterances be potent and factual so the words of your mouth and the meditations of your heart be acceptable to our maker to be rewarded.

I must say I really do appreciate your tolerance in this endeavor to read it, as wisdom is acquired from knowledge.

In my research for facts concerning the state this world is in, I have discovered that the cause for this entire world to be in a spiritual disarray is because of indoctrination. The instructional monument known as the bible that contain all the rules, instructions and directives is infected with inconsistencies too numerous to mention. The bible concluded centuries ago at the book of revelation. At this moment in time there's no evidence of any modern continuation in terms of directives, so the wicked adversary is in control.

We are existing in a danger zone and that's why the adversary is being elevated to being the god of this world that make it more evident that there are many other gods competing for our souls. It's compulsory for us all to wake up from our slumber and seek refuge in our maker by way of Christ and not in the names of Jesus and his mother Mary. Please do not ignore these facts as they are potent and meant to be concealed by the evil forces.

The entertainment industry is getting deficient of resource that it's accustomed to so several of the entertainers are resorting to the religious industrial complex becoming Christians. They aspire getting wealthy similar the popular pastors on TV and others, majority of the popular TV evangelists are millionaires, from my seat in the reality arena I vision them as being parasites, feeding on the tithes, offerings and donations from the unfortunate and disadvanted ones among us.

This planet earth is a posession of God and the fullness thereof including humanity. Seasons comes and seasons go based on timing as the globe revolves on it's axis. There are trends and things to be accomplished, choices to be made, places to go and other people to see. Life is a gifted previlage on a timer and predistined from inception to extinction. We humans are not the only species in the life process, as there are animals, flying things, insects, pestilence, mammals, fishes in the seas and others.

Another major component in the process are the elements of nature that sustains us that's extencive. As time goes by every opportunity I get to relate with someone concerning the things of god, I'm either rejected or debated. Recently I encountered a minister of a certain religion and I requested his tollerance by assuring him that I'll listed to his views and respect them also. I respect the bible but do not quote from it as in my research of the facts concerning our being I encounter inconsistencies in it.

The humans body is very complecated and consist of numerous systems operating in sequence, we consist of a body, heart, spirit, being and soul. While Jesus our savior was here on earth as a mortal human, he consisted of the same components we all contain as mortals. He was sustained by the trinity while doing the will of the father and did'nt become a spirit until he was resurected and transformed.

If you are observant you'll see me mentioning in the prior paragraph of the first earth and wonder if I'm loosing it, I will declear to you that I'm not. The original perfect earth created by God was poloted by Lucifer and had to be cleansed by water while the people of God were conveyed by Noah in the ark to dry land. As predicted we are presently living on the now earth extremely poluted by the evil adversary again.

Question, "How could we have existed without the bible?" It's the only holy history book in existence containing all the laws, rules, regulations, guidelines from our sustainer. God in three dimentions is an invisible spirit that exists in the realms of glory. He can be deserned, he sees, listens, responds, blesses, supplies, corrects, keep records and more, he does not utter or document.

All these actions are executed through inspirations by humans beginning with Jesus when he was in the flesh. The determination can be made that God is the author of the bible but no one owns it's copyright, God did have an influence on the content but it was done through several contributers by way of inspirations and acts of nature. They were all humans and we all have different views, opinions, assumptions, sugestions and predictions. The will of God must be done and he uses us based on the capability of our intellect.

Religions have decleared that the bible is the words of God, the most popular version is the King James version. There are sixty six books in it and the name of God was mentioned only once by David in the book of Psalms. Lord was a title that was given to Christ and was used as a substitute for the father Jehovah. Most of the other books were compiled with valuable substance from contributers of several professionals including presumptions that have been accomplished.

I did mention earlier about the different earths and due to the distructive agenda it's been operated under by the influence of the evil adversary, eventually there will be a final cleansing this time by fire. The new earth will be eternal paradise consisting of only spirits. As it was stated by Christ through Jesus's mouth that a place is being prepared for us his possessions to be with him.

Process is the beginning of existence, every process require resource to enhance productivity. Waste is the end product and without action there can be no result. The Lord / God is the main source that sufices the existence of humanity. The only holy history book known as the bible stipulate that the fear of the Lord is the beginning of wisdom. Although that book is the main guidance for human existence it's detrimental to pursue it's directives word by word.

Documenting the contence of the bible was an assignment given by God to various participants and their personal opinions are included in this book. How can we fear the owner of the breath that we breathe?, Wisdom is acquired from accurate knowledge documented in literature. That's why it's of vital importance to indulge in reading potent literature, of course you have to utilize the filter as there are disguised inaccuracies.

Christianity implicates followers of Christ and that's the correct and only way to communicate with the father at the throne of grace, not in the name of Jesus or his mother Mary. I'm sharing with you the results of my research for the truth, you do have the right to disagree. By grace we are saved as long as we accept and submit our being and be washed in the blood of Jesus, for the remission of our sins. Jesus is affiliated with the trinity but not a member of it.

Humanity need to wake up and concentrate more on the main source of our existence instead of Jesus as there are religions that worship Jesus as God. Although the bible is presented to us humans as the word of God the name of God is rearly mentioned, as a matter of fact the name Jehovah is mentioned only once in the bible by David at Psalms 83:18. What needs to be done is to take the emphasis off Jesus and concentrate more on the father and his commandments.

Almighty God in three dimentions centuries ago had one of his servants document ten commandments as directives for humanity to obey and abide by. Instead of promoting compliance of them religions do the opposite by defying them to the point where they are rearly mentioned. Yes we love Jesus and greatly appreciate all that he has done for us, whatever he accomliished was an assignment given him by the father on our behalf.

Time and time again he mentioned that it's the father that sent him here, after he completed his assignments the father was well pleased to the point where he begotted him as a second son. Eventually he will rule with Christ in eternal paradise on a cleansed earth. The bible joined him with Christ where it would seem that Christ is his surname, and religions use it as a tool to satisfy the evil adversary.

The word begotten seperate Jesus from being a fourth member of the Godhead so he is not God as God consist of father, son and spirit all being original neither created, made or born. Please be observant and desern that Jesus is the only begotten son of the father, the word begotten is similar to being adopted. The father shelters us his people in times of storm from his place in glory, while religions have people praying to him in heaven in Jesus name.

The word God is a title in three dimentions to the highest degree there is no other title higher, he have never been human. All of god's utterances were done by humans through inspirations even before Jesus came and were all documented and compiled into one book known as the bible. God originated and dwell in glory, not in heaven as taught by religions. Heaven is not a place of refuge it's one of the planets in the universe occupied by spirits including Jesus.

This USA consist of the most devisive religions and churches per-vapita than anyother place on this earth. The end of time is no where in sight as there will be other generations, it's imperative to concentrate on now. We are running out of our alloted amount of time and need to get on the right hi-way by trusting in the correct Lord. My assignment is to keep insinuating that Christ is the true Lord and the only way to eternity, assisted by Jesus.

Religions scare people by saying the second coming of Jesus is near, I will declear that he is already here omnipresently in spirit doing the will of the father. My appeal to everyone is to take the emphases off Jesus and concentrate on God, pray to him through Christ and not in the name of Jesus. Each of the three members of the trinity of God have names, Jehovah is the name of the father, Christ is the name of the son and Holy is the name of the Spirit.

It's been mentioned several times in the bible that holy is a ghost, that's another error in the bible as ghosts are spirits of the dead. Anytime you read the bible and see the names Jesus Christ, Christ Jesus, or Lord Jesus do put a conjunction between them as they are seperate spirits. Lord is not a name it's a title of God mainly used by Christ as he is the true Lord and the light of our salvation.

Anyone that aspire being in the secret place of the most high will be protected in the hands of the Almighty, like a hen sitting on her eggs to keep them warm. The implication that God's kingdom will come on earth as it is in heaven is reffering to paradise, it's being prepared for precious souls. Let's make a joyful noise unto the Lord and get in his presence with singing sweet songs of praise.

Hearts have been broken and soft words have been spoken to heal them, we as God's possession must give him thanks and praise contiually. The compensation process is alive and well, do not indulge in wrong deeds as the penalty can go to the fourth generation. It's more benificial to do good deeds with compassion to set up treasures for your decendants to achieve when the time is right.

Hopes, dreams, wishes, promises and gain are all promises that contain a degree of uncertainty. Always concentrate and be positive and anticipate the best from our main source of existence. Seek potent and accurate knowledge from literature to acquire wisdom to impact our being. It's of vital importance that we keep our minds active by generating positive thoughts to sustain our capabilities to produce substance.

The human brain have the capability to curtail negative influences in the process of obtaining vital substance from our sences. Of cource there's no perfect human so there are times when we bypass the approval from our hearts and make wrong decisions. Because the evil adversary have access to our mental faculties we must be careful and not allow ourselves to become volnerable. I must complement you on tolerating me to this point in this process.

I must instill in you that a need is more important than a desire and it is a one way street to acquire satisfaction, it is imperative that we always consult our heart before getting to that stop sign.

Be Redeemed By The Blood

The joy of the Lord is our strength, may we all that love the Lord join in a song with sweet accord and let our joy be made known in the beauty and spirit of holiness. Glory is a domain of God and the dwelling place of the most high in three spirits, one trinity. There is no other spirit that have the privilege to intrude in the realms of glory. Jehovah our father is the king of glory, open your hearts and let him in. Procrastination is a virus, Christ is at the door to let you in when you get cleansed by the blood of Jesus.

Holy the spirit has the authority to keep that entrance secured, be sure to get your name written in the lamb's book of life. I will reiterate that every time I mention God and Lord, it entails Father Jehovah, Christ the son and Holy the spirit all three spirits in one. I'm blessed to acquire my surname and got inducted in the hall of grace, not by myself but by the power of the spirit of God within me. I have dedicated my being to be utilized by God as a vessel to convey the good news of the redemption to the entire world of humanity.

I pledge from the bottom of my heart to continually bless the Lord with all that is within me until my last breath. The main thing I desire of God and that I seek after with prayers and supplications to eventually dwell in eternal paradise with Christ and Jesus empowered by Holy the spirit. As humans we operate by polarity similar to a battery our being we are positive and the negative is the evil adversary and his forces.

The product of the preceding combination is called emotions and if not controlled will liquidate to become tears. There are tears of joy and tears of sorrow, it is beneficial to be in total control of our emotions utilizing a high degree of tranquility, than allow them to supersede our happiness. The calendar specifies seven days but in our minds there's only three, yesterday today and tomorrow. Yesterday is in the past and tomorrow is promised to no one. Today is the day that the Lord give us and we must rejoice and be glad in it.

The bible is one of my favorite spiritual and history books but based on the irregularities I discovered in it, I have concluded that it's not totally the words of God as projected by religions. The most popular translation of the bible is the King James version and the total mentioning of God was substituted by the title Lord. The true name of the father is Jehovah and it's mentioned only once by the psalmist David. I respect the bible as there's no alternative as to the rules, guidelines and regulations and spiritual directives

It's not my intent to get involved in any form of controversy, debates of confrontation concerning the things of God. Here I will disclose two misconceptions surrounding the birth of Jesus our savior and redeemer, an angel showed up and inform them that " Unto us is born this day in the city of David a savior who is Christ the Lord" Christ the Lord was already here. Another angel declared that Jesus's name will be called " Mighty God, everlasting father, prince of peace and king of kings" The Almighty God Jehovah was there.

Jesus did come in the flesh and accomplished the will of the father whereby the father was well pleased in him and made him his only begotten son similar to an adoption. He conquered death and was ascended to heaven to join Michael and the heavenly host, the first thing he did was to revoke the passport of Lucifer and changed his name to Satan so he no longer have access to heaven to deceive the angels. Jesus mostly assist Christ in the acts of being an executer and representative doing the will of the father.

Religions try to issue scares for humanity to put up shutters like there is an hurricane on the horizon. There will be no second coming of Jesus on this earth because he is already here Omni presently in spirit guiding and preparing us his people for paradise. Ever since I started the pursuit of the pathway I choose to travel in life, nature have intervened and impacted the process by interacting in amazement. One bright summer day when the skies were blue with a few clouds, suddenly it changed to grey as I was sitting by my partially closed window.

Eventually it started to drizzle lightly and a single drop landed on my hand, of course I'm aware of the evaporation process. I commenced a conversation with that drop of water as if I was responding to a message it brought me, it then disappeared then down came a heavy down pour. Immediately I was implanted with inspirations that led me to approach the throne of grace by way of Christ. Of course the father is always there to greet me and respond to my supplications based on his promises. I will admit that spiritual meditation is one of my daily routine.

Although this may be a reiteration, It's my responsibility as a visionary messenger to let the facts be made known. Religions were devised and implemented by the evil adversary, shortly after the beginning of time and the first one was Catholicism. People were told that they can ask Mary the mother of Jesus to pray to God for them. Us here in the western world do celebrate the birth of Jesus in the month of December the final winter month of the year when the weather is chilly.

During that period of time there are numerous rituals and one of them is the process of cutting a tree, install it in residences and decorate it with lights and other ornaments. I did a research and discovered that was a practice of paganism in an early era where they exalted and praised Lucifer. The motives have been adjusted but it's now being a celebration of the birth of Jesus. There is another where a man is dressed up in red and white clothing with a beard that in most cases distribute the gifts that accumulated under the tree.

There are other traditions like exchanging presents and gifts and enormous amount of varieties of foods. Since the word Christmas included the word Christ in it, I became curious as I thought it was a spiritual occasion. I did a research of the bible and the word Christmas was nowhere to be found. Christ is the root word for Christianity and it's captured and utilized by religions as a name tag for the members.

I will disclose another reiteration with no apologies, Christ is a member of the trinity of God and is Lord, Word and son of God. At the birth of Jesus there was an announcement made by an angel that unto us a child is born in the city of David a savior who is Christ the Lord. The word beginning implies timing. God created the universe containing all the planets including heaven and earth, he then put only the earth on a timer in rotation on its axis. All the other planets are stationary.

Time started at zero and God in his entirety was present, they had a conference between themselves and made the decision to create two humans only one male and one female. All of us humans are made through a process, the first human was made from the dust of the earth. When the time came God's will was done for humans to inherit the earth and accomplish his mission. Jesus was absent from all those accomplishments and was born as a son of man by way of being a fruit of a virgin's human womb.

The birth of Jesus was long after the beginning in the year four thousand. Jesus originated by the process of Holy the spirit extracting a seed from Christ the Lord a member of the trinity of God and injected it into Mary. That was the moment when that seed became flesh to dwell among humans on the earth to accomplish God's mission. Religion teaches that Jesus was from the beginning as the word and was God, that's totally incorrect. Christ the Lord, God and Word have never been an human on this earth that committed sins and had to be baptized.

The period mentioned in the bible known as the beginning was when the clock started ticking and it does until this day. The rotation of the earth is based on a twenty four hour basis and do change periodically. Due to the rotation of the earth when it's night here it's day on the other side of the round globe, the brilliant glow of the sun, moon and stars do impact our existence and the water cycle and nature also. The morning and the evening was the first day and was named Sunday, one of the commandments of God for the world to obey stipulates the following.

It says six days we must labor and rest on the seventh day and keep it holy, at this moment in time religions don't even mention the ten commandments in their place of worship. I have submitted my entire being to God to be utilized as an instrument of his peace to impact the entire humanity in heading in the right direction to have a personal relationship with the father by way of Christ, the only empowered by Holy the spirit. The evil adversary designed religions to be an industrial complex and it's competing with other industries on the high end.

Last time I checked the zeros have exceeds nine. The appointed leaders especially those involved in multimedia are wealthy. There are leaders out there that travel in their own private jet planes at the expense of the unfortunate ones among us. Recently I learned of a ninety two year old male that was put out of his place of worship due to shortage in his tithing. It's setup that when the leaders require funds it's deducted from the tithes and offerings and when anyone in the congregation is in need they are sent to ask God in prayers and supplication's.

There is a popular entertainment celebrity that recently got saved, by what? I assume it's by the bell. This man eventually got himself a massive synagogue decorator with crosses and images of the assumed Jesus. This is how he operates it, he hire different preachers to deliver messages at different intervals and charge the members a fee. That fee is for entering to participate in worshiping to their father in heaven in the name of Jesus. I'm sure he makes the evil adversary happy as he is a false god. Neither God or our savior Jesus is for sale but religions are using the name Jesus as a commodity.

Christ is not the surname of Jesus, us humans are all an individual unit with the mental capabilities of making our own choices and decisions. The initial command is to seek first the kingdom of God and righteousness for all things will be awarded to us. There is only one true and spiritually living God, but how the evil adversary designed it make them all divisive as all religions although they use the same bible and differentiate according their belief system. Recently I discovered that there is a religion that identify themselves as witnesses of Jehovah the father.

It is becoming frequent for the formation of new religions with catchy name brands to attract the vulnerable ones among us. The preceding scenarios are for real and are disguised, I'm sure the information disclosed in this publication will get officials in high places in religion upset including their god. I do have a large following on social media where I share my seventy years of personal experiences and the inspirations I obtain during my daily meditations. I'm not interested in any confrontations, debates or biblical corrections.

Recently I was accosted by one of the followers in my audience and got to realize that he is a religious bishop. He accumulated a list of books, chapters and verses from the bible ready to accost and correct what I post on the net. I explained to him where I'm at in the process of my assignment to penetrate the entire humanity with the facts of our spiritual destiny. Recently I managed to do an assessment of my name Noel Grace and was amazed at what I discovered based on spiritual potency and credibility.

Jesus was the first Noel it's specified that it's by grace through faith we are saved by Jesus's blood, and grace is the preservative for wisdom. The acknowledgement of Christ is the beginning of wisdom, it's beneficial to establish a personal relationship with the father. In order to communicate with him we must go in by the only way, through Christ at the throne of grace. Faith is an ingredient that's rarely mentioned and it's essential to counteract deceptions. Father we enter your gates with thanksgiving and your courts with praise.

All of us humans are individually made as a unit with the mental capability of discernment and comprehension to make the right decisions and choices. A lack of wisdom create vulnerability to cause default in the equation of survival. If we make wrong choices or decisions we will suffer the consequences and if we make the right ones we'll reap the benefits. Every action me take in deeds have a reaction, credibility is a vital element to be compensated. Always be sure that our utterances are truthful and credible, if we acquire any loans be sure to repay it according to its terms.

Endeavor to choose compliance over complications as the latter can be problematic, as there are catchments set up in the system of things to capitalize from it. At this time in the pursuit of my life there's nothing more substantial than exploring the source of our existence. I'm convinced that God is using me for his purpose based on the inspirations he's implanting in me. I'm presently at a point where my curiosity is going wild whereby my exploration for facts have intensified. It's my intent to continue sharing my findings with you my international audience.

I do appreciate if you'll join me in spreading the good news to all the world, I'm aware that the evil adversary and his forces are obstacles in our pathway. In my department of the process of life, the virus called stress cannot intrude my mental faculties to deter my mission. God is the ruler of our destiny and overlook the valley of distress and wants to supply our needs in abundance according to his will. I was inspired to do the following in order to clarify that's there are several spirits.

I'll do this illustration from a practical intimate prospective, say me and my brother were walking on the road to school. My name is James and my brother's is John, up came a bus that stopped and the driver instructed the conductor to allow James in for the ride and John his brother ALSO. Does that mean both brothers become one? the answer is no. Jesus the messiah and savior of our souls requested that all humanity believe in God and believe ALSO in him.

Based on my capability of discernment, I comprehend that Jesus and God are separate spirits because the same conjunction ALSO implied is the same that was between James and John. Based on our acceptance of Jesus as our savior from sin both inherited and committed, it's of vital importance that we get washed in the cleansing blood of the lamb of God. Once that is accomplished we are destined when the time comes to be changed in the twinkle of an eye. We will be destined to be with Christ and Jesus in eternal paradise.

The wages of sin is death, what does it profit a human to gain all the treasures of this world and loose his soul to the evil adversary who is destined for destruction in the lake of fire. Behold how good and pleasant it is for us all to dwell in the peace of God, we must seek first the key to the way to paradise and all things necessary will be awarded to us by God. Praise God from whom all blessings come, praise him continually anytime and anywhere we are here on earth. We must exalt him above the heavenly host and let his light shine in us to expand his kingdom.

Life does have its seasons, always be prepared to weather the storm and rely on the promises of God as they are sure. Do not allow the dark clouds of today to impede the brilliant glow of a brighter future, father we give you praise. Try to do everything in moderation as abuses causes early extinction from life. When someone dies that's not it, there's another realm to go to with dual compartments, be sure to be on the right tract to eternal paradise.

It is eminent that you'll see something mentioned more than once in this publication as repetition is the adjective by which substance get attached to minds. Please overlook typographical errors and misplacement or absence of letters. I'm absolutely certain that there are facts disclosed here that's aware of but I'll assume that other writers are scared to disclose them as it's detrimental to the system of things.

Culmination

Never get involved and be affected in anyone elses pain or sufferings, only sympathize and offer assistance if you can. Due to the compensation factor they may be paying the price for something they did or inherited from the past. The bad deeds done in the past can cause consequences to the fourth generation. Plant a seed by investing in a human being and you will be rewarded accordingly in due season. What does it prophet a man to gain the whole world and loose his valuable soul to be acquired by the evil forces automatically.

My advice to you is not to be selfish, it's more rewarding to indulge in generosity than being parasetic. Sharing is caring and like blossoms that bring fruits of blessings to be achieved by us. Always insist that your commtments be credible, it's always best to be punctual on appointmants and adjust your space in society to accomodate others. Our body is a massive entity of enormous capabilities, never under estimate it's power and motives in the process of survival. Play close attention to the flags our bodies wave called symtoms, as they are whistles blown when services are required.

Always seek professional help and log into the main computor for directives and protection. Be causious of what we digest in our stomach, it's benificial to indulge in the consumption of the natural rather than the processed. A name denotes identity with attachments and of no other significance, it's not like a key to access doors of previllages. It's a known fact that the train of life is moving right along one day at a time and the older we get is the faster it seem to go.

It's an amazing experience being an author because we develop the capability of absorbing substance from numerous sources to be documented in the process of completing a project. It's similar to being a sponge or a magnet waiting to absorb material substance to cause an impact. In order to materialize the thing we aspire to accomplish we must be able to identify them by way of desernment.We should always be positive and associate with people with high asperations, doubt and fear are deterrents to progress.

Presently we are existing in times when there are people drowning in adversities of circumstances they created by making defective decisions. Due to this advercity it's becoming rear that we see someone with a smile on their face indecating happiness in their state of mind. Recently I was in a convenience store and observed a female projecting all the right qualiies in her demeanor of a very happy person and that's very rear.

I did not see her as attractive externally and she was not all dressed up with the usual make-up, false hair and all the other stuff that usually attreact the eyes of males. As a male of course I could'nt resist but to get engaged with her in a conversation to complement her for display of her state of mind. Her responce was as if she thought I was trying to make an advance on her. She said thanks for the compliments and disclosed that the reason for her actions was because she saw her husband drove by.

Lots of people waste time complaining about situations without realizing that they are in full control of their life within the boundries of the laws that they have to comply with. Never seek advice from your pears as some human's tendencies are like that of crabs, whereby if they identify your advancements they will try to pull you back. There are people that are deceptive by convincing others that they are able to predict their future, only God know what the future holds.

Variety is a spice of life and that's the reason why I have given you the opportunity to utilize my gestures to awake your mental faculties to the realities of our duration of this life. I will assure you that the conents of this publication will impact your life positively and worth your investment in acquiring it. In this system of things we try our best to make a living and forget to live. The preservation of our sanity is vital to our existence and the impact it create will benifit future generations.

Our existence rely on resources and there are numerous different forms depending on our location. Because there is an issue or population explosion it's imperivive to mass-produce to keep up with supply and demands. Import and export are healthy for commerce in the distribution of goods between different nations and provide employment for employees. In my section of the US there is an influx of people from South America with different languages. My neighbor is from Brazil and speak three languages Spanish, Purteguese and English.

It's benificial to seek and discover your tallents and potentials in order to access and utilize them to the maximum. The heavest load you can convey with your mind is a grudge, if for any reason your spirit and someone elses negatively colide it's best to avoid contact. We must realize that the world consist of all kinds of people, there are people that enjoy making other people unhappy. I will assume that those kind of folks have problems falling asleep at nights, different strokes for different folks.

Before you go to sleep at nights allways endeavor to give thanks and praise to our maker and sustainer, expressing to him your appreciation for having another day of life with all it's blassings and press the delete button to dump the past. Dreams are real most people give up or lost them, never give up on them there is always the possibility of having them fulfilled. In this life it's benificial to set goals and consistently work toward achieving them.

If at anytime you lack the courage to innitiate a project you already lost, never stand in the way of achieving your own success. There are dreams you acquire in a unconscious state of mind while sleeping. Those are being prossessed by your subconscious mind working overtime and in most cases they are illusive. There are also day dreams that are more practical, as they can be materialized based on our desires to accomplish them.

The contents of this media was designed to make a signal to the world as to the derection in which we should be going in so we can achieve our gift. I will consider this book unusual as it causes you to get to the point of awareness concerning the existence of our being and beyond. If you are observant you would have seen my mentioning of that place being prepared by Christ with Jesus to accept whoever chooses called paradise.

It sure will be a glorious accasion we will be changed to be spirits in the twinkling of an eye and the dead in Christ will join us. The original intent of this media is to devise and impliment a monument of change in the revolutions of human cosscious minds. I've done much to impact yours and wish you all the best on the basis of the following.

1. Happyness will keep you sweet.
2. Trials will keep you strong.
3. Realities will keep you humble.
4. Success will make you flurish.
5. Only the breath of God can keep you alive.

The Author

The author is a visionary messenger and realistic indevidual that sees life as a practical voyage to an ultimate destination. Although it's obvious that there will be obsticles in the pursuit, realizies that in order to reach the right destination we must jump over the hurdles and persistently stay the course. Many have previously tried and failed but the journey of life goes on, until that time when we access the new spiritual realm.

I will confess to you that I will miss your presence in absorbing my implications. Humanity was placed here on this earth to fullfil a purpose, seek your tallents and utilize your potentials to the maximum. Stand on the promises of God because they are sure, keep his commandments and you'll be rewarded.

Hope to encounter ya'll in paradise.

Noel G. Grace

Printed in the United States
By Bookmasters